WIRRAL WALKS
100 miles of the best walks in the area

Anthony Annakin-Smith

Published by Sigma Leisure – an imprint of
Sigma Press, 5 Alton Road, Wilmslow, Cheshire SK9 5DY, England.

British Library Cataloguing in Publication Data
A CIP record for this book is available from the British Library.

ISBN: 1 85058 823 6

Typesetting and Design by: Sigma Press, Wilmslow, Cheshire.

Photographs: by the author except where indicated

Cover photograph: Denhall Quay, Little Neston (from the 'Little Neston and Ness' walk).

Maps: Bute Cartographics. Maps for Walks 2 to 7 inclusive and 11, 12, 18, 19, 20, 22 and 25 reproduced by permission of Ordnance Survey on behalf of the Controller of Her Majesty's Stationery Office ©Crown Copyright. Licence number MC 100032058.

Printed by: Bell & Bain Ltd, Glasgow

Foreword

by Mike McCartney: Cultural Ambassador for Wirral

Those of us who live on the Wirral realise how fortunate we are in having such an interesting and varied landscape so close to home. If we want to explore open spaces we can choose the contrasts of farming country or beach; marshland or heath; woods or parkland. Walking doesn't only help us see the Wirral – it's also a great way to shed those extra pounds and look after our hearts. And if we want to delve into Wirral's rich cultural history we can find places with links to prehistoric man, through thousands of years of history up to the development of industrial England. It is a privilege to be Cultural Ambassador for an area of such diversity.

Furthermore, what makes Wirral particularly special is that all this heritage and culture is so easily accessible, in fact right on our doorsteps! We have an excellent network of footpaths and other walker-friendly routes just waiting to be explored. But that's for us Wirralians ... we're OK, but are you one of the lucky ones?

And where to walk? As luck would have it, all our problems are solved with Anthony Annakin-Smith's book of 'Wirral Walks'. Not only does it suggest some great walking routes but it also explains what we can see along the way, bringing Wirral's scenic and historic heritage to life.

I am sure you will enjoy using this book and wish you many happy hours exploring the rich landscape that Wirral has to offer. If I bump into you en route, don't forget to say 'Hi'!

Yours walkingly

Mike McCartney

Preface

I hope this book will appeal to two kinds of people.

First, if you're someone who just wants a refreshing local walk but doesn't know where to go, it suggests routes to follow – 25 in fact. These range from those that are suitable for parents with young children to full-day ones for more adventurous walkers.

Second, if you're the type of person who's curious about what you see along the way, it aims to answer the kind of questions you might ask. Why are there so many ponds on the Wirral? What made them put that lighthouse there? When was that rock carving made? Why are there so many village names ending in 'by'? Who decided to put a fifth clock on that church tower? And so on. In this respect, I hope that armchair readers can get as much from the book as walkers.

For me, walks prompt a never-ending series of questions. I hope this book will answer at least some of yours.

Acknowledgements

If you like this book it's probably because so many people helped me to write it – in lots of different ways. These include:

Rodney Wright and Jen Lewis for their inspirational teaching and leadership on the Diploma in Landscape Interpretation at the University of Liverpool. Hazel Clark, Jo Crossley and the Department of History team at Chester College also deserve a mention.

The countryside rangers at Leasowe, Hilbre, Thurstaston, Royden Park, Eastham, Rivacre, Dibbinsdale and Hadlow Station, employed by either Wirral Borough Council or Cheshire County Council. They were invariably very helpful and full of good information.

Dennis Tomlinson, the author of 'West Kirby and Beyond – An RAF National Serviceman looks back' (Ameliel Press), price £8.50, for kindly allowing me to reproduce the photo on page 64.

Many other people helped in different ways. In particular I should mention Paul Loughnane, Rusty Keane, Gavin Hunter, Mike McCartney and Chris Holbrook. Also, those who allowed me to use their photos – names are given alongside the photos, where appropriate.

Thank you also to the many people of Wirral who contributed but whose names I never knew. Not one person ever objected to being in a camera shot, offering information or (occasionally) letting me onto their private land.

Finally thanks to Ruth for proofreading and to Ruth and my children James and Claire for 'road-testing' the walks and for allowing me the time to write all this!

Anthony Annakin-Smith

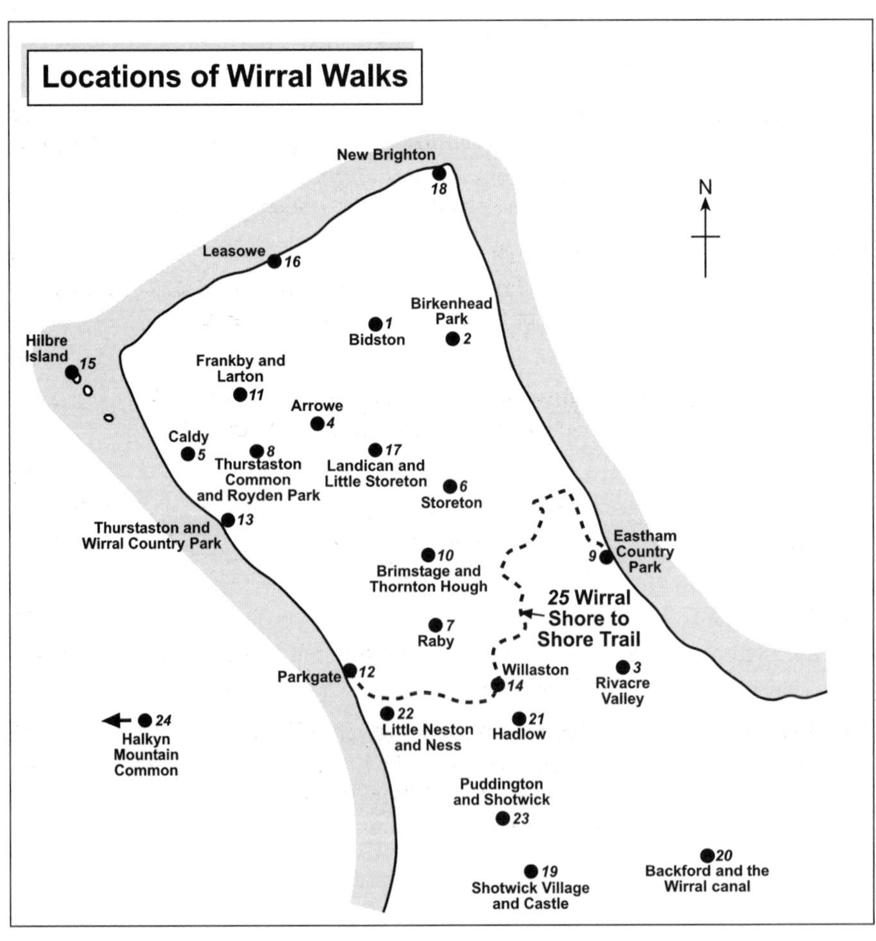

Contents

Introduction 1

The Walks – in ascending order of length

Walk 1. Bidston 4

Giraffe food – woodland and heath – a windmill – a children's farm – ancient rock carvings – maritime history – old buildings

Distance: 1¾ or 2¼ miles; allow at least 1½ hours

Walk 2. Birkenhead Park 9

Parkland – wildlife, including wildfowl to feed – unusual buildings

Distance: 2 or 2¾ miles; allow 1½ or 2 hours

Walk 3. Rivacre Valley 15

Country crafts – a one-time major tourist attraction – meadow – wildlife – woodland – wood carvings

Distance: 2 miles or 3½ miles; allow 1 hour or 2 hours

Walk 4. Arrowe Country Park 21

Waterfalls – wildlife – parkland – woodland – sites of historic interest

Distance: 2¼ or 3½ miles; allow 1½ or 2 hours

Walk 5. Caldy 27

Heathland –fine views – a pretty village – a beach

Distance: about 2½ miles; allow 1½ hours.

Walk 6. Storeton 32

A tramway line – quarrying – Roman connections – the Forest of Wirral – harsh penalties for law breaking – a former racecourse – woodland

Distance: 2½ miles; allow 1½ hours.

Walk 7. Raby 37

A former racecourse – pretty woodland – fine views – an ancient village

Distance: Just under 3 miles; allow 1½ hours.

Walk 8. Thurstaston Common and Royden Park 42

Views – meadowland – a miniature railway – woodland – Thor's Stone – heathland – Hillbark House

Distance: 3 miles; allow 2 hours

Walk 9. Eastham Country Park 48

Woodland – river views – sea-life sculptures – a former pleasure gardens and zoo – Mersey ferry crossings

Distance: 3¼ miles; allow 2 hours

Walk 10. Brimstage and Thornton Hough 54

Farm-pet animals – craft centre – wildlife – an environmentally friendly farm estate – historic villages

Distance: 3½ miles; allow 2 hours

Walk 11. Frankby and Larton 60

Parkland and farmland – giraffe food – a former RAF camp – a tree plantation – old farming methods – traditional buildings

Distance: 3½ or 3¾ miles; allow 2 hours.

Walk 12. Parkgate 66

A former ferry and fishing port, and seaside resort – disused railways – coastal walking – saltmarsh – wildlife – great views

Distance: 3½ or 5¼ miles; allow 2 or 3 hours

Walk 13. Thurstaston and Wirral Country Park 72

A waterfall – beach walking – wildlife – the Wirral Way – Ice Age cliffs – a rail accident

Distance: 3¾ miles; allow at least 2 hours

Walk 14. Willaston 79

A restored railway station – a Roman road – old buildings – Wirral's largest windmill – an ancient hedge – the Wirral Way – farmland – glow-worms

Distance: 3¾ miles, allow 2 hours

Walk 15. Hilbre Island 84

Great views – an old lifeboat station and signal station – rock caves and an arch – wildlife including seals – a weather station you can check at home – the site of dinosaur prints

Distance: about 4 miles; allow 1 hour each way, plus stops

Walk 16. Leasowe 90

A lighthouse – a hovercraft tale – coastline – sand dunes – hay meadow

Distance: up to 4 miles; allow at least 2 hours, but easy to shorten

Walk 17. Landican and Little Storeton 95

Ancient lanes – an air crash site – farmland – pretty hamlets – a puzzle for cyclists – old buildings – old farming methods

Distance: 4 miles; allow 2 to 2½ hours

Walk 18. New Brighton 100

Street art – a one-time entertainment mega-resort – coastal walking – a lighthouse – a pretty park – the Liverpool Bay oil and gas rig

Distance: up to 4 miles; allow at least 2 hours

Walk 19. Shotwick Village and Castle 106

A medieval castle site – an unspoilt village – a visit to Wales – the changing Dee estuary – woodland – farmland – ancient buildings

Distance: 4 or 4½ miles; allow 2½ hours

Walk 20. Backford & the Wirral Canal 112

An historic road – a canal, boats and bridges – old buildings – farmland

Distance: 4¼ miles; allow 2½ hours

Walk 21. The 'Lost Village' of Hadlow 118

A 'lost' village – Roman, medieval and turnpike roads – a restored railway station – farmland – unusual trees

Distance: 4½ or 5¾ miles; allow 2½ or 3 hours

Walk 22. Little Neston & Ness 124

Wirral's only coal mine – disused railway lines – a deep railway cutting – ancient lanes – woodland – saltmarsh – the Wirral Way

Distance: 4½ miles; allow 2½ hours

Walk 23. Puddington & Shotwick 130

A menagerie – ancient villages – a large pigeon house – the medieval landscape – redwood trees – masons' marks

Distance: 5¼ miles; allow 2½ to 3 hours

Walk 24. Halkyn Mountain Common 136

Mining landscape – an Iron Age hillfort – great views – a different perspective on Wirral – quarrying – lime kilns

Distance: 6½ miles; allow 3 to 4 hours

Walk 25. A Wirral Shore-to-Shore Trail: Parkgate to Eastham 143

– A fine route right across the Wirral –

Distance: 10½ miles for the full walk. Otherwise, split the route into two or three sections for a series of outings.

Introduction

These walking routes first appeared in *Wirral Essence* magazine. Over the four years they were published, I was encouraged to receive so many comments from people who had enjoyed them – both walkers and 'armchair ramblers' who enjoy *reading* the routes as much as *treading* them. Several people suggested compiling the routes into a book and this is the result – but I have included more material than was in the original articles.

For me, one of the many pleasures of walking – besides the fresh air, great scenery and health benefits – is learning about the landscapes we so often take for granted. This book has given me the opportunity to say much more about the fascinating features of those landscapes than space allowed in the originally published routes.

The Wirral Landscape

The landscapes we see on Wirral, and elsewhere, do not just 'happen'. They are created by a variety of factors acting with or against each other. Man has shaped the landscape for thousands of years. It is surprising how many signs of medieval, Anglo-Saxon, Roman and even prehistoric people we can find in our area, as well as numerous signs, of course, of more recent events. To a large extent, man's activities have been driven by the local geology – the rocks and soils underfoot are constant reminders of Wirral's more distant past. And these rocks and geological conditions, together with other factors such as the weather, have combined to create a huge range of environments to support different plants and animals. I have aimed in this book to look at all these different factors and see how they have shaped the local landscape. Having said that, if there's 'too much information', just relax and enjoy the walk for its own sake.

A word about equipment

If you are not used to country walking you may be unsure what you need. My general advice is to keep it simple, with one or two exceptions. Wherever you are walking on the Wirral, you are never going to be very far from civilisation. There is usually likely to be a road, track or building within a few hundred metres so there's no need to go equipped for a major expedition. The sands between West Kirby and Hilbre are a major exception and I really would not recommend these in poor visibility.

Perhaps the biggest local hazard you need to be prepared for is mud. Several of the walks are on dry ground but for others you need to be ready for mud – especially if you are walking in winter and/or crossing farmland.

My basic advice is:

Maps – recommended but not *essential* on any of the routes, as the maps in the textbook should give you all the key information. If you are walking in poor visibility then a map is often valuable (provided you know how to read it!). Having said that I *always* carry an Ordnance Survey map, at 1:25 000 scale – just because it can answer lots of questions about the landscape. The Wirral map is no. 266 in the Explorer Range. For Walk 24, across Halkyn Mountain Common, use no. 265.

A compass – not usually essential, for the same reason. If you are walking in poor visibility though, a compass is essential. Once my wife and I did a complete 360-degree circuit of a field without realising it, in thick fog, as we didn't have a compass!

Footwear – if the 'Walking Conditions' at the start of each route says there may be mud then be ready for it – especially in winter. This means having good waterproof shoes or preferably boots. Wellies are not ideal for walking in but are often practical if you expect very muddy stretches, and are often best for children.

Refreshments – a bottle or two of liquid will seldom go amiss, and are certainly recommended on hot summer days. Plenty of liquid is essential for the longer routes i.e. Halkyn Mountain and the Shore-to-Shore, and recommended where there are no other refreshments available e.g. on Hilbre Island. Most of the other routes can be accomplished in half a day but why not take a picnic anyway and make a day of it? In addition, a supply of sweets helps keep energy levels up – and are great motivators for reluctant children!

Clothing – wear whatever is comfortable but bear in mind that, if a walk takes two or three hours, the weather can change substantially in that time. Take waterproof jackets if rain is forecast. The Hilbre Island and Halkyn Mountain walks can be quite exposed, so have warm clothing available – the weather may be warm at home but could be cool and windy along these routes.

A walking pole (woe betide you if you say a walker is holding a 'walking stick'!): again, far from essential but having said that, I wouldn't be without mine. My wife and I stopped counting the number of uses we had put it to after about number 30. These range from testing the soundness of footbridges to retrieving maps that have blown into trees! Oh, and they take a lot of stress off your joints too.

The Countryside Code

We are lucky to enjoy such superb countryside but it takes care to keep it that way – care by landowners and by users. We all have a responsibility to look after the countryside, and the Countryside Code summarises what we should all do:

✓ Be safe – plan ahead and follow any signs

✓ Leave gates and property as you find them

✓ Protect plants and animals, and take your litter home

✓ Keep dogs under close control

✓ Consider other people.

For more information, see the official website: www.countrysideaccess.gov.uk/countryside_code. If you want to be more involved with preserving our local footpaths then why not join the Wirral Footpaths and Open Spaces Preservation Society? Their website, www.wirralfootpaths.org.uk gives much more information.

But that's enough from me. You didn't buy this book for a long Introduction – so on with the walks!

Walk 1. Bidston

Giraffe food – woodland and heath – a windmill – a children's farm – ancient rock carvings – maritime history – old buildings

Start and finish: car park by Tam O'Shanter Urban Farm, signposted off the B5151, Boundary Road.

Distance: 1¾ or 2¼ miles; allow at least 1½ hours, plus time at the farm.

Refreshments: at Tam O'Shanter's Farm.

Walking Conditions: woodland and heathland paths – mostly dry but occasional muddy patches after rain which are usually easy to avoid; some uneven, rocky surfaces. One optional short climb.

This is a short walk, but allow plenty of time as there's so much to see around this lovely area of heath and woodland.

Start with a visit to Tam O'Shanter Urban farm – open daily from 9.00 to 4.30, free of charge. There are plenty of animals as well as an interesting activity room, a Treasure Hunt course and a Nature Trail. Take time to look at the thatched cottage, with its stone carving of Tam O'Shanter fleeing from a witch across a bridge. Also the new Ecobuilding, which has walls made of straw bales and a roof covered with the alpine plant 'sedum'.

1. Take the track marked "Permissive Horseride to Upton Road" between the car park and the entrance to the Farm.

2. At a wide path turn right for 50 metres; then turn left, immediately after the picnic bench, to enter the wood. Take the first path to the right, to go through the wood.

This is Taylor's Wood, a 9-hectare woodland. It has a lovely feeling of openness, and is dominated by Scots Pine, with its characteristic red bark higher up the trunk. You are sure to see grey squirrels scurrying around.

3. Go past the left-hand end of an old stone wall, and almost immediately onto a path of exposed sandstone. Bend right towards the windmill, eventually crossing a bridge.

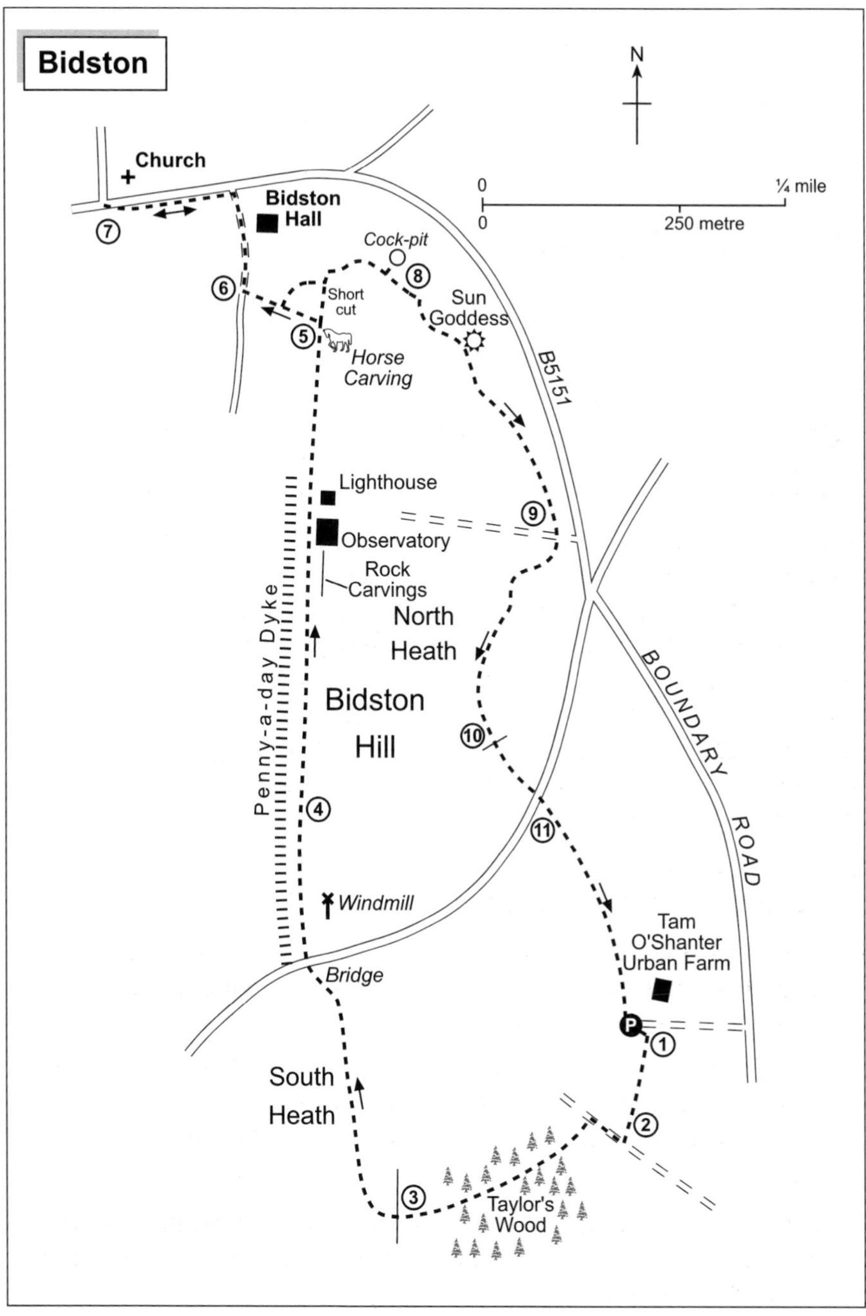
Bidston
N
Church
Bidston Hall
0 ¼ mile
0 250 metre
Cock-pit
Short cut
Sun Goddess
Horse Carving
B5151
Lighthouse
Observatory
Rock Carvings
North Heath
Penny-a-day Dyke
Bidston Hill
BOUNDARY ROAD
Windmill
Tam O'Shanter Urban Farm
Bridge
P
South Heath
Taylor's Wood

Bidston Mill

From the wood you enter an area of heathland. Heath is characterised by thin soil, lacking in nutrients. Typical plants include common heather (as well as other types of heather), spiky gorse whose yellow flowers have a characteristic coconut smell, and silver birch. In fact, birch is so abundant here that some of it has been cut and crushed, and then used to feed giraffes at Chester Zoo!

The windmill was built around 1800. It replaced one that burnt down when a gale turned the sails too fast, causing friction that started a fire.

The old mill was situated 30 metres north of the current one and was rotated into the wind by the miller pushing on a wooden arm sticking out near the base. Two oblongs you can see carved in the rock were anchor points for the brake of the mill's turning mechanism; 3 metres further north are carved footholds used by the miller to help him push the wooden arm. A Bidston miller was once killed when he stepped out of the mill and was hit by one of the sails (which were longer than those seen today). On another occasion a tinker's donkey that was tethered to a sail flew into the air when the sail rotated – it survived!

5 metres later, on the opposite side of the path, there is a round post-hole in the rock. This was one of many on the ridge, used from the 1760s, to hold poles for flags giving news to Liverpool merchants of incoming ships so they could get ready for unloading.

Later, a series of high-level semaphore signal-stations was established at Bidston, Hilbre and along the north Wales coast – messages could be passed along the chain of signal-stations from Anglesey to Liverpool in eight minutes.

4. Continue along the ridge to Bidston Observatory.

Immediately before the Observatory you may like to drop down the steps by the wall. To your right is a vertical face of sandstone on which you can find carvings of two human figures and a horse.

There used to be an astronomical telescope in each of the Observatory's two rotating domes. Later, it became the Liverpool Observatory and Tidal Institute, calculating tide times around the world and inventing the first electric tide-predicting machine. The Institute played a key role in predicting tides for the World War II D-Day landings in France. Now the site is disused and, at the time of writing, its fate is unknown.

The wall to your left is called Penny-a-day Dyke and was built 600 years ago as part of the boundary of a deer park which stretched down towards the River Fender. Its builders were paid one old penny (about ½p) per day.

This lighthouse was built in 1873 but is no longer in use. This, and its predecessor, was used in conjunction with Leasowe Lighthouse (Walk 16); when the two were in alignment it indicated the entrance for ships to the Rock Channel which led towards Liverpool's docks.

Just before point 5 you walk over an area of flat sandstone. Take a few moments to study it and you will make out a carving of a horse – it was once 3.5 metres long but is being increasingly worn down and now only the head is really clear. Its origin is unknown.

5. Follow the path as it turns left and drops downhill. (For the short cut, continue straight ahead, passing a stone gatepost to your right, along a narrow path overgrown with holly and rhododendrons. Emerge between points 7 and 8.)

6. At the bottom of the hill, turn right and visit Bidston village, a Conservation Area.

Bidston Hall was probably built in the early 1600s. Not only is the grey sandstone building impressive but it also has a magnificent raised gateway. The Hall is said to have once been lost and won in a game of cards; a summerhouse was subsequently built in the shape of the ace of clubs.

There are many fascinating buildings in the village made from the same local stone. These include Church Farm, which has 13 different floor levels; Stone Farm (by the letterbox) – a former inn known as the Ring O' Bells which was linked to a local smuggling network; The Lilacs, with its tiny windows; and, opposite, Yew tree Farm, dated 1697.

7. Retrace your steps to halfway up the hill you previously descended. Go left opposite 'Coote Hill' and immediately fork left to cross a small open area. At the far side, continue straight ahead and uphill. At the top of the hill, go straight ahead.

After about 75 metres look for a narrow path on your left just before a bank with an oak tree on it. This leads to a circular area called the "Cock-pit". Its origins are uncertain but it may have once been a mill for grinding gorse for animal feed; it is thought to have then become a site where illegal cockfights took place.

8. Retrace your steps and continue along the path.

By the house, look for a wooden post marking the Sun Goddess which is carved into a flat piece of sandstone. She faces exactly east, towards the rising sun on mid-summer's day, and is thought to have been carved by Norse settlers around 1000 years ago. Continue on the path downhill.

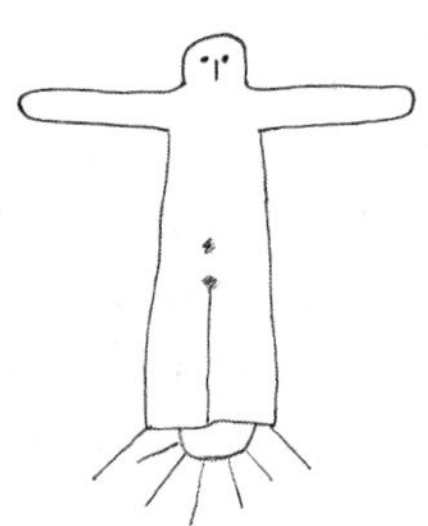

The Sun Goddess

9. Cross the tarmac drive to the Observatory, taking the narrow path ahead.

10. At a break in a ruined wall, follow the horseshoe sign to the left.

11. Cross the road. After 150m, go through the gap in the fence to take you back to the car park.

Walk 2. Birkenhead Park

Parkland – wildlife, including wildfowl to feed – unusual buildings

Start and finish: Corner of Park Road East and Park Road North, Birkenhead.

Refreshments: none in the Park

Distance: 2 or 2¾ miles; allow 1½ or 2 hours

Walking Conditions: level tarmac paths throughout, suitable for wheelchairs, pushchairs etc.

If you are not familiar with Birkenhead Park, you might be surprised by its story and the variety of its scenery. If you do know it, you will already appreciate how it offers a little oasis of tranquillity in the urban sprawl of Birkenhead and its surroundings. Either way it offers the opportunity for a gentle stroll with plenty to see. If you have children, taking bread to feed the birds on the lakes – including swans, moorhens and mallard ducks – is a 'must'!

You'll notice that the parkland is generally very flat. This is because, until the 1840s, this area was just marshland. However, prompted by a government initiative to create better recreational facilities for people in the growing towns of England, a local man, William Jackson, had the visionary idea of creating a park for the public's use. Nowadays we take parks for granted, but making a purpose-built publicly funded park that anyone could use was a new idea in early Victorian England.

1. Go through The Grand Entrance, made from sandstone quarried at Storeton (Walk 6). Continue ahead to the Jackson Monument, dedicated to the man who was the driving force behind the Park.

2. Go right for 10 metres, then left to pick up the lakeside path, going anti-clockwise.

This path constantly curves as do most of the other paths, and the banks of the lakes. The designer of the park, Sir Joseph Paxton, wanted to create a 'countryside' feel with open meadows,

The Lower Lake

meandering waters and scattered trees. Just as in nature, you will find few straight lines here.

There are likely to be fishermen around the lake – it holds many types of fish including pike, roach, bream, carp, chub and tench.

3. Reach the Roman Boathouse, which once held rowing boats for hire. Climb the steps and admire the pebble mosaic, laid in 1990.

Continue, and after a few metres you will see the Swiss Bridge to your left. Originally, you could walk on it but now it's inaccessible and spans two islands.

Look for a grassy gap between the trees to your right. Immediately after this gap, on a bank about 3 metres away from the path, is a 'black mulberry' tree with its distinctive gnarled, reddish-brown trunk. In late summer, the tree produces mulberries, which are similar to raspberries, and which you will find scattered all over the path. Next time you sing the nursery rhyme 'Here we go round the mulberry bush …', you'll be able to picture one!

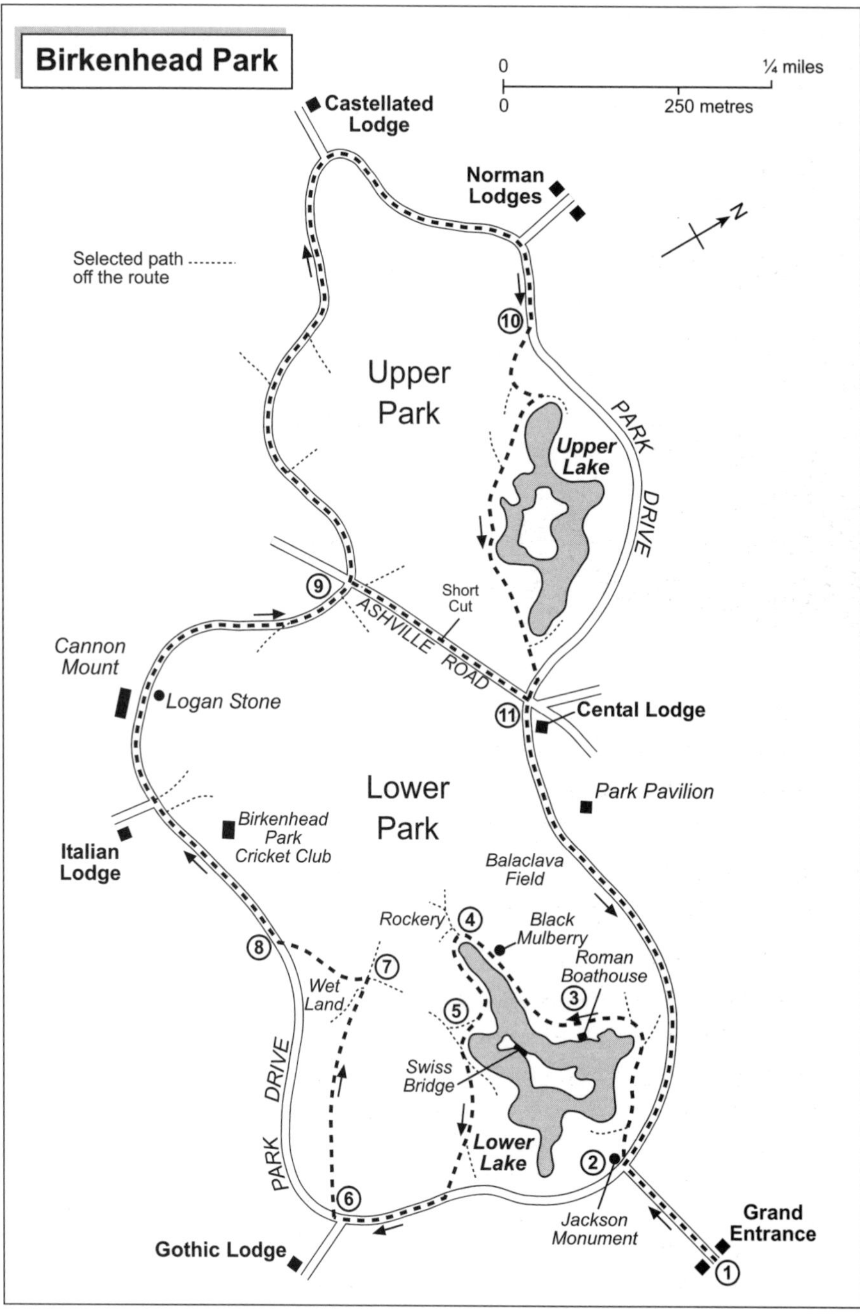
Birkenhead Park
0
¼ miles
0
250 metres
Castellated Lodge
Norman Lodges
N
Selected path off the route
10
Upper Park
Upper Lake
PARK DRIVE
9
Short Cut
ASHVILLE ROAD
Cannon Mount
Logan Stone
11
Cental Lodge
Lower Park
Park Pavilion
Birkenhead Park Cricket Club
Italian Lodge
Balaclava Field
Rockery
4
Black Mulberry
Roman Boathouse
3
8
7
Wet Land
5
Swiss Bridge
DRIVE
PARK
Lower Lake
2
6
Jackson Monument
Grand Entrance
Gothic Lodge
1

4. Continue to the rockery, made of sandstone slabs, popular with clambering children.

The park's designer, Paxton, dug the lakes and used them to drain off some of the water from the marsh on which the park was built. He used the material excavated from the lakes to form the small hills throughout the park which break up the flat landscape.

In 1850, three years after the Park opened, Frederick Olmsted visited it. He went on to design Central Park in New York and said he drew many of his ideas from Birkenhead.

5. Stay on the lakeside path past a grassy mound between a triangle of paths; at the next fork, continue straight ahead to reach the perimeter road – Park Drive. Go right.

Horse-drawn carriages once paraded along this wide track, leaving the inner parts of the Park safe for pedestrians.

In the corner of the Park note the first of six Lodges, built in different architectural styles. This is the 'Gothic Lodge'.

6. Turn right, down the narrower path between lime trees. These were planted in 1953 to mark Queen Elizabeth's coronation. Continue to a cross-paths in a slight dip.

7. Go left. After a few metres, there is a wetland area to your left.

This was meant to be the Park's third lake, but became a shallow wetland habitat as it never retained sufficient water.

8. Continue ahead reaching Park Drive, and pass the tented pavilions of Birkenhead Park Cricket Club.

The pavilion was opened in 1993. Creating areas for people to play sports was part of the grand plan for the Park from the start. Birkenhead Cricket Club was formed in 1846, in anticipation of the opening of the Park.

100 metres after the pavilion you can see the impressive 'Italian Lodge' by the gates to your left.

Soon, at the top of a gentle rise, you see a pillar – the Logan Stone – marking the holding here of the 1917 Welsh National Eisteddfod

The Castellated Lodge

(there was once a large Welsh-speaking community each side of the Mersey). Interestingly this stone, placed in England to mark a Welsh festival, is made of granite from.......Scotland!

Immediately before the Logan Stone is a large property, Cannon Mount, one of many Victorian properties around the Park's edge. When the Park was created, about 40 hectares (100 acres) of perimeter land was set aside for building plots, the sale price of which more than paid for the Park's construction.

9. At Ashville Road turn right for the short cut, or cross the road into the quieter Upper Park. Stay on Park Drive to reach the 'Castellated Lodge' with its castle-like features. Continuing on the main track, you pass the two 'Norman Lodges' after about 250 metres.

10. Fork right onto a narrower path 75 metres later and take the first path left to join another lakeside path, anti-clockwise. Fork right at the end and cross Ashville Road again (note the unusual Victorian pillar box to your left) and pass the 'Central Lodge'.

11. Continue on Park Drive back to the start.

You will pass a new Park Pavilion on your left. This is one element of a five-year restoration scheme for the Park, part-funded by the Heritage Lottery Fund. At the time of writing, the Pavilion was far from finished but, just as Jackson's and Paxton's ideas were futuristic, so also (according to Wirral Council) will the new Pavilion be in its use of materials and its approach to the environment.

To your right is Balaclava Field, named after the famous battle in the 1850s Crimean War where the Charge of the Light Brigade occurred. Two Russian cannons captured in the War once stood on Cannon Hill.

Victorian pillar box near the Central Lodge

Walk 3. Rivacre Valley

Country crafts – a one-time major tourist attraction – a peaceful meadow – wildlife – woodland – wood carvings

Start/finish: Rivacre Valley Country Park

Refreshments: Poole Hall Country Inn, near point 3; Ellesmere Port Golf Centre bar may be open for drinks and snacks.

Distance: 2 miles or 3½ miles; allow 1 hour or 2 hours.

Walking Conditions: Generally easy walking, often on firm paths. Some woodland stretches may be muddy after rain.

This corner of Wirral is often overlooked, but this is a lovely walk through several deciduous woodlands, besides streams, and along a meadowy valley that feels miles from anywhere. An unusual feature of the route is the opportunity to see examples of some ancient woodland crafts.

Rivacre Valley Country Park covers over 160 hectares (400 acres) and forms part of The Mersey Forest – an initiative covering large parts of north Cheshire and Merseyside creating new green spaces, woodlands, ponds, hedges and meadows.

1. Take the path to the right of the rangers' cabin, and turn left at the top of the steps. Continue ahead when a path joins from the right.

   The field to your right once offered an attraction of national interest – an outdoor swimming pool set in beautifully landscaped rose gardens. People flocked from far and wide to bathe in the Olympic-sized pool, opened in 1934, which was filled by water pumped from the Manchester Ship Canal a mile away. It closed in 1981 and the hole was infilled leaving no sign today. There are photos on the noticeboard you pass. Look out for a rectangular concrete area along this path – there are several holes where metal pipes once emerged, probably into a shower block.

2. At the path T-junction, turn left through a gap in the wooden fence. Go straight ahead with houses on your right. When the path swings right, go straight ahead, across grass, aiming for a wooden fence on the far side of the field, slightly downhill.

Look at the low-set hedge to left and right just after the metal gate, this side of the ditch. This was made as part of a national 'hedge-laying' competition in 2004. Hedge laying is an old craft involving almost completely cutting through healthy stems, which are then bent over horizontally. Surprisingly the process encourages strong growth, and helps to form a secure barrier. (You may find it hard to see the laid stems when the hedge is in leaf.) See photo on page 56.

3. Turn round and from the gate take the tarmac path downhill. Just before metal gates turn right down the tarmac path.

4. At the bottom of the hill, fork right and cross a wooden footbridge over Rivacre Brook to enter Well Wood. A few metres later turn left on a gravel path.

Have a look into the woodland ahead of you just before you turn left – many of the hazel bushes have been coppiced. Under this ancient practice certain types of trees and bushes are cut back to their base, typically every seven years. This encourages new growth in the form of several shoots rising from the stump to make straight and sturdy poles. These have many uses including fencing.

In spring this area is carpeted with bluebells.

The building foundations you pass on the right once housed a well used by Bowaters paper manufacturers to supply water to their nearby factory. A surviving example of the building can be found at the road.

5. Cross the road (Take care! Traffic can be fast here). Go right for a few metres, then through a wooden barrier, to join a tarmac path through Clayhill Wood. Continue to a bridge made of railway sleepers, crossing it.

About 150m after the road you pass an elm tree growing next to a large stump on the left. This is one of the most important sites in the Park – the upper branches are home to the rare white-letter hairstreak butterfly.

About 20m before the bridge you may be able to spot several small

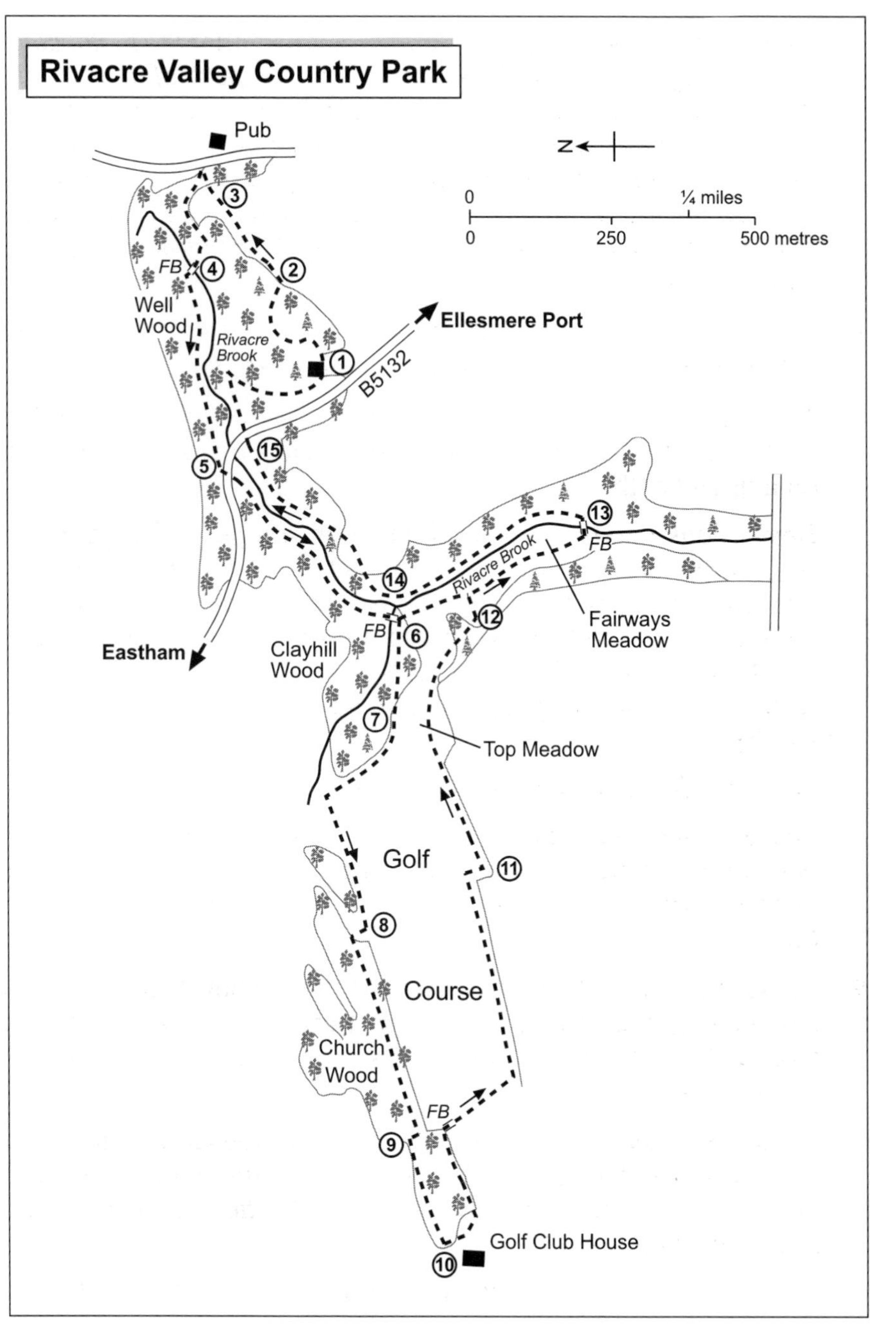
Rivacre Valley Country Park
Pub
N
0
¼ miles
0
250
500 metres
Ellesmere Port
B5132
FB
Well Wood
Rivacre Brook
Eastham
Clayhill Wood
FB
Rivacre Brook
FB
Fairways Meadow
Top Meadow
Golf
Course
Church Wood
FB
Golf Club House
1
2
3
4
5
6
7
8
9
10
11
12
13
14
15

holes in the far side of the stream bank (though you probably will not be able to if the banks are covered with summer vegetation). These are kingfisher nests and, if you are very lucky, you may get a glimpse of this iridescent blue bird darting along the brook.

Bulrushes

6. A few metres later, at cross-paths turn right to go uphill. (For the shorter walk, continue straight ahead at the cross-paths to enter a valley shortly after point 12 below).

7. A few metres after the bench near the top of the hill fork right along a grassy path to reach a golf course. Keep to the right-hand edge of the course, through a gap in a chain-link fence. Stay on the good path for 50m to a hedge and turn left to walk with the ditch on your right.

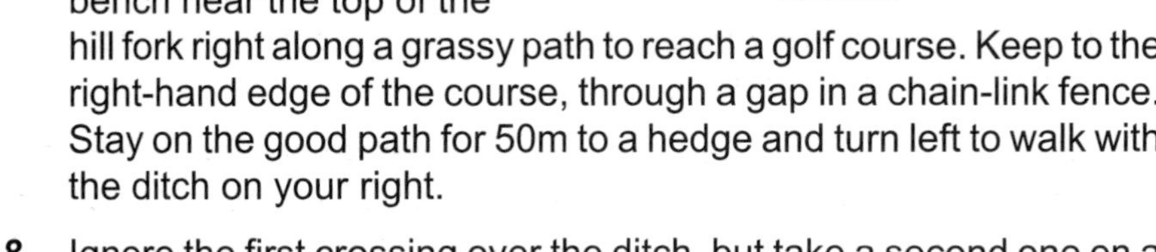

8. Ignore the first crossing over the ditch, but take a second one on a good path. However don't follow the path round to the right but go straight ahead into woodland through overhanging trees. A few metres in, pick up the obvious path to go left through Church Wood.

   This is a lovely path but beware of tree roots which present plenty of trip hazards!

9. The path eventually swings right and comes to a path-junction. Turn left and continue straight ahead between ponds to right and left, through woodland

   The ponds are marl pits – see page 99.

Fairways Meadow

Eventually you get an impressive view of the large and ornate St Paul's Church, Hooton.

10. Reach a car park. Immediately turn hard left, almost doubling back on yourself (note the map set on top of a boulder to your left). Join a gravel path at the end of an open area, re-entering the wood. 150m later go right to cross a bridge made of railway sleepers. Continue straight head, keeping in the same direction to reach a fence corner. Turn left.

After a while the path goes sharp right. On your left, on the golf course, are two sandstone blocks below oak trees – they look like old boundary stones but I haven't yet worked out what the lettering carved on them stands for.

11. Reach a cul de sac – but stay on the wooded path. Later, just after a metal gate on the right, take a path that forks to the right, swinging away from the golf course. At the red brick wall, continue ahead.

12. After 100m, when the view opens up to the left, look for a totem pole and drop down using a narrow path that passes it. At the bottom, turn right.

The totem pole is decorated with various symbols relating to Ellesmere Port including the 'Mersey Forest' tree and the emblems of Shell and Vauxhall.

This lovely valley is managed as meadow. It is called Fairways, giving away the fact that it once formed part of a golf course. The meadow is cut late each year after the seeds of the flowers and grasses have fallen, ready to provide next year's growth. You may wish to detour left, to the valley end, to see the information board that tells you more about the flora of the valley.

13. Walk for about 250m, passing a sea serpent carved in a log. Look for a path forking left, over a footbridge. Cross, and turn left again to walk alongside Rivacre Brook.

In places where the bank is eroded you may see short sticks of willow pushed into the mud. These 'willow pegs' will soon take root, helping to stabilise the soil and prevent erosion by the brook.

14. Later at a footbridge, do not cross but turn right, staying on the main path. 100m later, at an open area, fork left passing right of a picnic bench. Pick up the path on the opposite side of the clearing. Follow it to the road.

15. Go straight across the road; after 200m take a concrete path forking right and soon go right again uphill. Continue back to the car park.

100m or so to your left as you climb the hill is the 'International Woodland' made up of tree species donated by many countries worldwide. Stop on the hill to admire the superbly carved wooden seat.

Walk 4. Arrowe Country Park

Waterfalls – wildlife – parkland – woodland – sites of historic interest

Start and finish: Car Park on Arrowe Brook Road (which branches off the road between Arrowe Park Hospital and Sainsbury's).

Distance: 2¼ or 3½ miles; allow 1½ or 2 hours

Refreshments: Cherry Orchard pub at the main entrance, and at Arrowe Park Golf Centre.

Walking Conditions: grass, tarmac, woodland paths, fields. Muddy in places – but the part most likely to be muddy can be avoided by using the tarmac track from the car park to point 3).

Arrowe is one of Britain's largest public parks – 172 hectares (425 acres), making it bigger than Hyde Park in London. Much of this walk is through deciduous woodland and it makes a fine route at any time of year, with varying leaf colour through the seasons and changing bird and animal life.

The park has many amenities and is popular with model aircraft flyers. Ranger services include guided walks, children's fun activities, natural history studies and orienteering. Call the rangers for details (at Royden Park: 0151-677-7594).

In 1985 the park was the scene of a much-publicised incident when the South-African-born runner, Zola Budd, was bundled out of the Women's National Cross Country Championships by protestors, injuring her jaw. Budd, a top 3,000-metre runner, had controversially been given British citizenship so she could represent Britain in the 1984 Los Angeles Olympics (sports' fans may recall that she came seventh in the Olympics after accidentally tripping up American favourite Mary Decker).

1. At the far end of the car park go though a gap in the wooden fence, aiming half-left towards a wooden post just visible by the trees in the distance.

2. Go through Gorse Covert. When you emerge, aim slightly left towards higher ground, to walk alongside a line of white poplar trees.

Sandstone pillar left from when the park was farmland

The little diamond shapes on the bark are typical of the white poplar. When the trees are in leaf, they seem to shimmer in the breeze.

The large open area around you was the scene of the 1929 Boy Scout Jamboree, attended by Baden-Powell, the founder of the scout movement (who found out he was to be Lord *Baden-Powell while the Jamboree was in progress). This was the 'Coming of Age Jamboree' as the movement was 21 years old, and 50,000 scouts came from 50 countries. There was a large central arena surrounded by a sea of tents one mile long. At the end of the meeting, Baden-Powell sent a message of peace from Arrowe, via his scouts, all over the world. From then on, the Golden Arrow became the Scout symbol of peace.*

3. Join the main tarmac path and follow it round to the left. About 75m after the old toilet block, at a 5-way crossing, turn right.

Opposite Arrowe Hall the tall conifers on your left are giant redwood trees. Touch the bark and you will find it is soft and spongy – not what you might expect from such mighty giants. In total, the park has 43 tree species, many rare, including four types of oak – pedunculate, sessile, turkey and red.

Arrowe Hall to your right was built in 1835 by John Shaw, a member of a wealthy ship-owning family which had made money

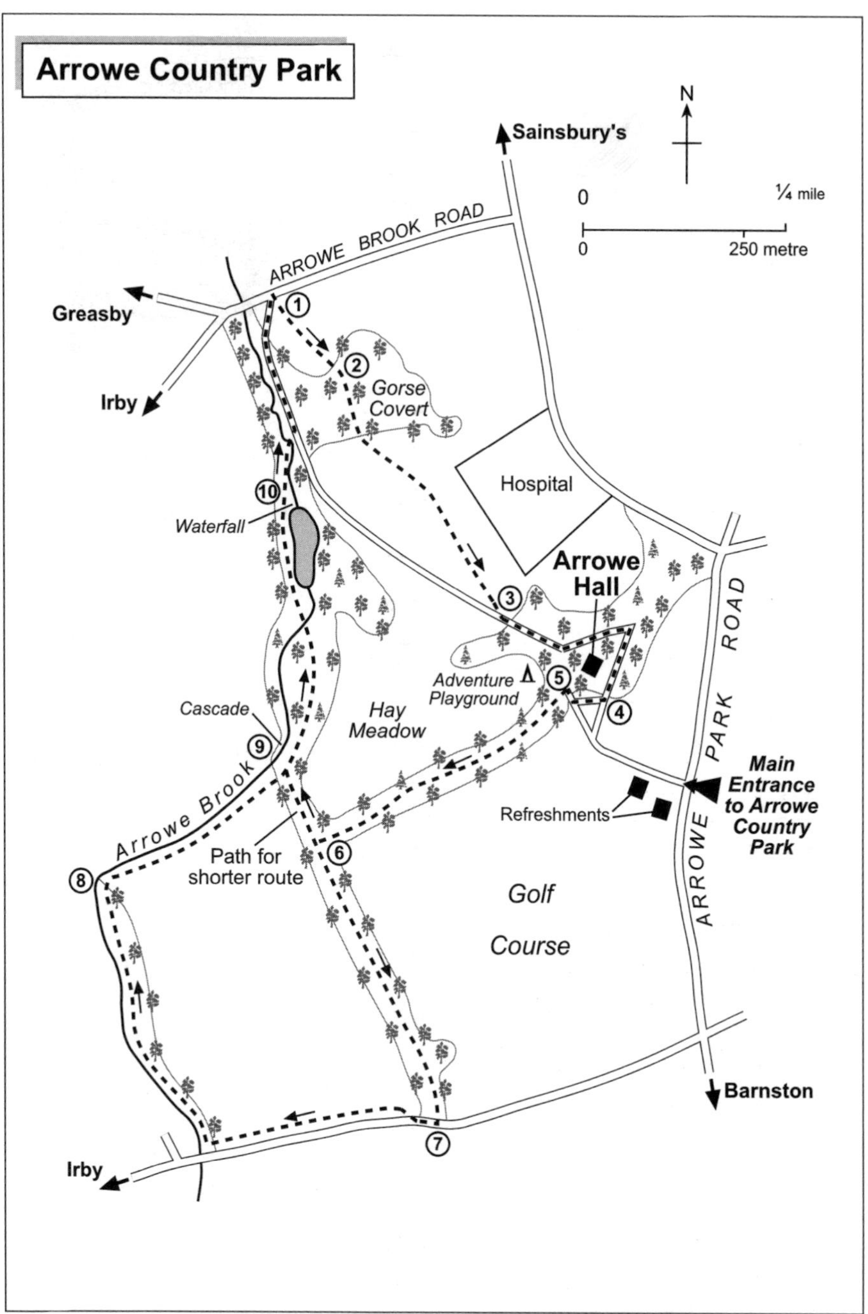
Arrowe Country Park
N
Sainsbury's
0
¼ mile
0
250 metre
ARROWE BROOK ROAD
Greasby
Irby
Gorse Covert
Hospital
Waterfall
Arrowe Hall
ARROWE PARK ROAD
Adventure Playground
Hay Meadow
Cascade
Arrowe Brook
Main Entrance to Arrowe Country Park
Refreshments
Path for shorter route
Golf Course
Barnston
Irby

from slave trading through Liverpool. The Hall was later enlarged to exhibit trophies, including nine tigers, from one family member's hunting expeditions. The building became a hospital during both world wars.

The land was later owned by Lord Leverhulme (who built Port Sunlight) who gave it to Birkenhead Corporation in 1926 for the 'enjoyment of the public'.

4. At another cross-paths just before a low metal fence on the left, turn right. Turn right again at the next junction a few metres later.

5. Cross a wooden footbridge; go immediately left onto a path through woodland. (Children will prefer you to go via the nearby Adventure Playground!)

There are ponds on both sides in this woodland. These are old marl pits – turn to page 99 for more information.

At the first track crossing the path take a short detour to the right to the stone gateposts. On the grassland there are some more, isolated, stone posts standing on the grass. When the Shaw family bought the land it was farmland and these surviving gateposts are left over from that time. In certain light you may also be able to see dips and troughs in the field – probable signs of old 'ridge and furrow' farming (see page 61).

Return to the main path and take a similar detour at the next crossing track.

The grassland here is managed as hay meadow. No pesticides are used, allowing natural growth of flowers and grasses. Each half is usually cut in summer in alternate years, with the other half left to grow to provide habitats for over-wintering animal life. You may see a kestrel hovering over the meadow, waiting to swoop on some unsuspecting vole or mouse.

To your left is the golf course whose ponds include the rare great-crested newt. The range of wild animals and plants is the reason why much of the park has been designated a 'Site of Biological Interest' (SBI).

6. At the end of the path, as it meets another, go ahead, over a foot-

Tha lake at Arrowe Country Park

bridge, through a gate, over decking, and turn left. (For the shorter walk turn right at the junction to reach point 9).

Note how this plantation has a healthy mix of trees of various ages. The numerous narrow ridges and dips were made when the trees were first planted, and would have assisted drainage.

Birds to keep an eye open for here include great spotted woodpeckers (if you don't see them you might hear their loud, rapid tapping as they bore into tree trunks); brightly coloured jays, nuthatches and treecreepers (nuthatches cling onto trunks and walk spirally downwards; treecreepers walk spirally up). Grey squirrels are everywhere!

7. Continue to a road, turning right along it for 600m. When the service road ends, turn right, signed to Arrowe Brook Lane, walking alongside Arrowe Brook.

The 'Riva 2005' sign on the fence relates to an initiative, now called 'Action Wirral Rivers', to improve the quality of local watercourses.

8. Just before you would cross a footbridge, turn right through a metal gate, signed 'Permissive Path'.

9. After three more gates you re-enter woodland. Go down and up the steps, then straight ahead to reach the main path after 25m. You will want to go left, but before you do ...

There is a lovely little water cascade on your left here. In summer it is just a trickle but, when it's wet, the water tumbles and splashes noisily down little natural sandstone steps. Keep an eye out for kingfishers along this streamside section, though these are more likely to be seen by early morning walkers.

Continue, eventually reaching a lake.

The lake, now popular with anglers after carp and bream, was made by the Shaw family who dammed Arrowe Brook. At the far end is a man-made waterfall (though if the weather's dry the water will not be doing much falling!).

10. Continue along the path you have been on, to join another, which takes you back to the car park.

Walk 5. Caldy

Heathland – fine views – a pretty village – a beach

Start and finish: Wirral Country Park car park near the bottom of Croft Drive, Caldy (to find it, from the A540 Telegraph Road follow the signs to Caldy; fork left after the church down Croft Drive. Go first right, continuing to the bottom of the hill).

Refreshments: two pubs towards the end of the route

Distance: about 2½ miles; allow 1½ hours.

Walking Conditions: Dry, sometimes uneven, paths, which may occasionally be overgrown with prickly plants.

This short walk takes in pretty Caldy village and the nearby fine lowland heath, as well as offering superb views. You may also like to visit Caldy Hill National Trust reserve, with more fine views, off the B5141 Caldy Road.

1. From the car park, turn left. Ignore Croft Drive West to the left but continue uphill and, as the road bends right, fork left up the signed bridleway.

The sandy conditions are typical of much of the walk, which is on sandstone. The stone, found in various shades, is used in local buildings, walls and The Mariners' Beacon that we will see later.

2. At the road, turn right and follow the main road through Caldy village.

The name 'Caldy' probably comes from old Norse words meaning 'cold islands' referring to a time when this area was included in the same administrative region as the Hilbre islands. Norsemen settled on Wirral shortly after AD900.

Carved stones date several buildings to the late 1600s and early 1700s. I particularly like the 1683 Manor Farm, made from huge sandstone blocks, covered by a sagging slate roof. In the 1830s, a wealthy Manchester businessman, Richard Barton, set about renovating local properties, creating today's 'chocolate box' village

Caldy village

centre. He built huge Caldy Manor, complete with clock tower, which you may hear chime.

3. Just before no. 109, Caldecot Cottage, turn left up the bridleway.

4. At the road, continue almost straight ahead, to the right of a telegraph pole.

This old path from Caldy is called Fleck Lane. There is a great variety of young deciduous trees here, encouraging plenty of songbirds throughout the year.

5. Stay on the walled route until 25m before the metal pole in the centre of path (and a white house shortly after it on the right). Go left through the break in the wall and immediately bear right, passing a leaning birch to your left, through rhododendrons.

Follow the clear path to open heathland. Keep right, continuing on the main path which seems to bear away from the coast. (Numerous paths criss-cross the heath, which can be tricky for direc-

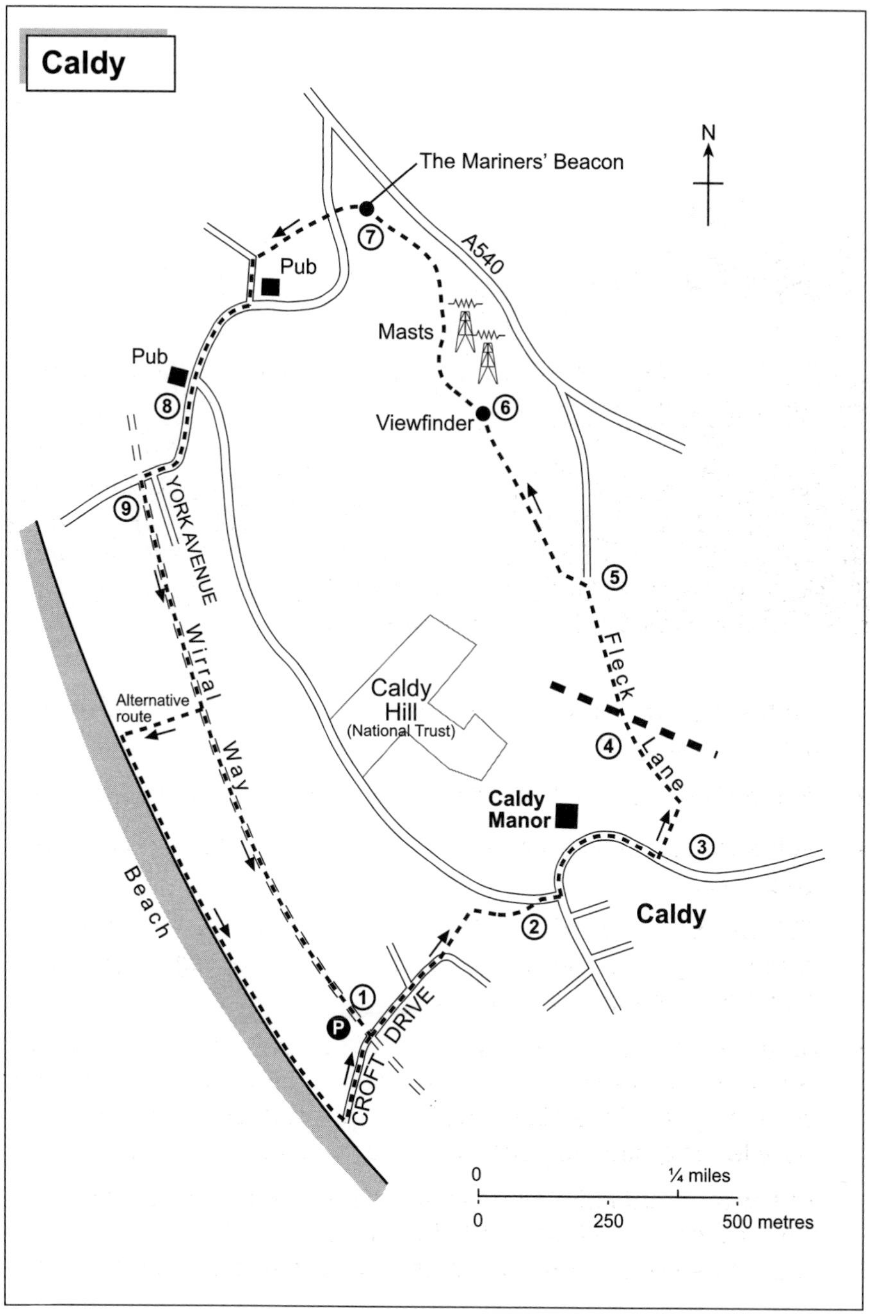
Caldy
N
The Mariners' Beacon
A540
Pub
Masts
Pub
Viewfinder
YORK AVENUE
Wirral
Way
Alternative route
Caldy Hill
(National Trust)
Fleck
Lane
Caldy Manor
Caldy
Beach
CROFT DRIVE
P
0
¼ miles
0
250
500 metres

tion-giving. As general guidance, stick to the main path; aim for the wireless masts which you will see after a while, and then the tall column with the ball on top).

Caldy Hill is an area of lowland heath. This type of habitat is threatened in the UK so the hill is very important. Heathland soils are typically poor in nutrients and only certain plants can put up with these conditions.

Three types of heather are found locally, the commonest is ling; there is also bell heather which has cluster of large bell-shaped flowers on the upper stems, and cross-leaved heather, found in wetter areas, with leaves that form a cross-shape when viewed from above.

You may also see clumps of bright green-leaved rhododendrons growing on the open heath. They are bad news! They are not a native British plant and have a habit of overwhelming everything around them so that the natural heathland plants, and the animals they support, disappear.

After 350m you will see a viewfinder mounted on a stone plinth to your left.

You are 79 metres above sea level here and the viewfinder is an excellent guide to the superb views. On a clear day, you can see Anglesey (47 miles away) and even Snaefell mountain on the Isle of Man (81 miles). Hilbre Island is visible to your half-right and, off the Welsh coast, the thirty wind turbines of the North Hoyle wind farm, Britain's first major offshore wind farm.

6. From the viewfinder, take the main path dropping down to the left of wall. Keep on the same general heading. In places where the path forks, take the right-hand, upper, path. Eventually reach the Mariners' Beacon.

Erected in 1841 as a navigation aid for shipping, this replaced a windmill that seafarers had found an invaluable landmark until it was destroyed in a storm 1839. The granite millstone at the base of the column came from the mill.

7. Go down the steps in front of the Mariners' Beacon. At the road go straight over, alongside a fence. At the next road turn left and, at the pub, turn right.

The Mariners' Beacon

8. After a second pub, the Moby Dick, turn right down Sandy Lane. 150m later at York Ave., descend the steps to join the Wirral Way.

The Wirral Way was opened in 1973, and was Britain's first designated Country Park. Previously it was a railway line, opened in 1886, enabling Victorian folk to start taking day trips to the seaside – this was long before the era of motor cars. It also made it easier to get locally produced goods to the towns and cities, including milk, grain and vegetables.

9. Stay on the Wirral Way back to the car park. Alternatively, for an open view, use the Wirral Way to start with but, after 500m, turn off right, across open grassland. Provided the tide allows, walk back along the beach to the breakwater. (N.B. the 'path' that runs above the limestone coastal defence boulders eventually peters out.) Climb the flight of steps and, at the top continue up the road back to the car park.

For information on the birds in the estuary, see Walk 15.

Walk 6. Storeton

A tramway line – quarrying – Roman connections – the Forest of Wirral – harsh penalties for law breaking – a former racecourse – woodland

Start and finish: rough ground by the black and white footpath sign in the centre of Storeton.

Distance: 2½ miles; allow 1½ hours.

Refreshments: none on the route but the Travellers Rest pub is at the top of Rest Hill Road by Storeton Wood.

Walking Conditions: Good tracks, roads; short sections of field-paths.

This gentle walk offers fine views over central Wirral and goes through the delightful Storeton Wood. This area was the site of stone quarrying for centuries and examples of Storeton stone engraved by the Romans can be seen in Chester Grosvenor Museum. You can see the stone throughout the walk, in boundary walls and buildings; it was much used in the local area e.g. for Birkenhead Town Hall, and was even used in the construction of New York's Empire State Building. It has a distinctive colour, much whiter than the red sandstone which you find elsewhere on the Wirral.

1. Take the track signposted 'To Brimstage'.

There was a steeplechase course between Storeton and Barnston, one of several former racecourses on the Wirral (see also Walks 7,12 and 16). A balcony on the rear of Lodge Farm was used as a viewing point for the races.

2. Go through the kissing gate and straight ahead. By the motorway cross a stile and follow a path to reach the road. Turn left.

3. As the road bends left, take the signed path ahead to Higher Bebington. Follow over another stile, then a footbridge. Now arc slightly anticlockwise, aiming uphill for a footpath sign to the right of the road ahead. Cross the sandstone stile.

This is Red Hill Road. Some historians claim that a massive battle

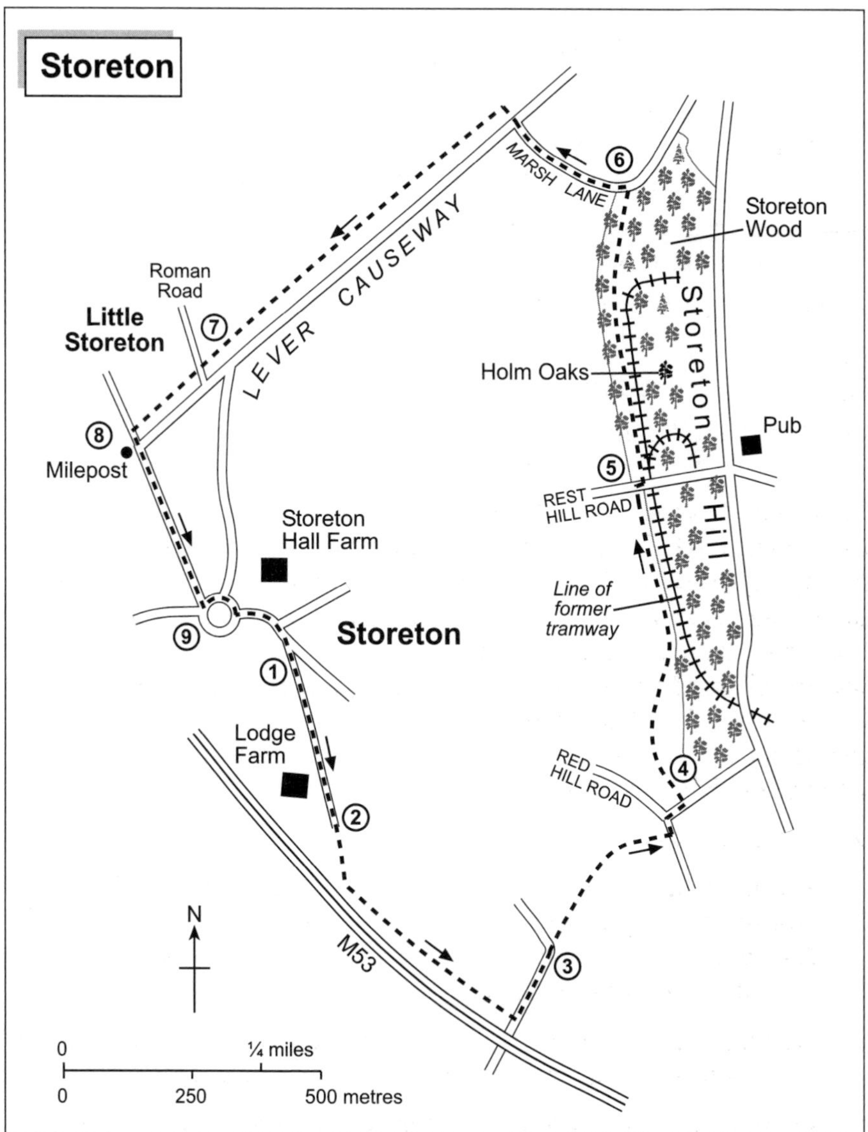

between Norsemen and Anglo-Saxons – the Battle of Brunanburh in the year AD937 – occurred on the Wirral, possibly on the ridge between Storeton and Higher Bebington. Folklore suggests that Red Hill was named after the blood that flowed down its slopes.

4. Take a signed footpath to the left, a few metres uphill, signed to Rest Hill Road.

5. Go straight ahead at Rest Hill Road. Our route follows the clear path, but you may prefer to wander through the woodland paths.

Amongst the wood's birdlife watch out for treecreepers, which climb spirally up tree-trunks, and nuthatches which, alone among British birds, walk down the trunks. There are also jays, lesser-spotted woodpeckers (listen for their loud drilling sound as they bore into the trees) and several types of butterfly. Holm oaks, planted at the edge of a clearing on your right after 200 metres, are evergreen trees with acorns that take two years to ripen.

The path is the track of a tramway, built in 1837 to take a stone to dock at Bromborough Pool. Horses pulled the tram trolleys along the horizontal sections of tram rail; gravity then let the trolleys roll down to Bromborough, with the speed controlled by a brakeman; the horses then pulled the empty trolleys back up the hill. The tramway went directly through the middle of the Lever Brothers factory site at Port Sunlight and was a source of annoyance to the Levers for years! You can see an example of the narrow tram rails 400m along the path.

The quarries (three in total) were higher up, near the main road, and were over 60 metres deep. They were mostly infilled in the 1930s by material excavated from the first Mersey road tunnel. You can still see some of their sunken outline today (you might like to wander up through the woods to see where they were). Fossilised tracks of dinosaurs were found 20m down in 1838, and the animals were given a scientific name based on the quarry's location – Cheirotherium storetonensis. Examples of the tracks, also found on Hilbre Island, can be seen in Victoria Hall and Christchurch, both in nearby Higher Bebington (incidentally – if I may go off on an outrageous tangent – the Beatles played Victoria Hall in 1962!).

6. At Marsh Lane, turn left to reach the Lever Causeway. Cross the road and go left.

This avenue was one of several created by Viscount Leverhulme,

Pushchairs now trundle where a tramway once ran

though most are on his private estate. They were part of his plan to build wide residential roads for the growing Wirral population and were to comprise a central road, with service roads each side. But with the coming of the First World War, the plan was never completed.

7. As the road bends left, go straight ahead down Little Storeton Lane into the pretty hamlet of Little Storeton.

'Roman Road' on your right wasn't named as such until 1938! It is certainly old, however, and was possibly linked to the Roman quarry work and the Roman road through Willaston (walks 14 and 21).

8. At the National Cycle Network milepost, turn left.

For more on the milepost, see page 96.

After about 150 metres you can see Storeton Hall Farm over the road to your left. Facing you is a high wall, with a blocked up window, forming the gable end of a farm building. This is the most

Storeton Hall Farm: the wall of the Great Hall is on the left

visible remaining section of a great hall, part of the original Storeton Hall built in the 1360s by the Stanley family. They were probably the most powerful Wirral family in medieval times and there are many tales of them abusing their position at the expense of the long-suffering ordinary folk.

Their power came from holding the position of Chief Forester of Wirral. Wirral was a royal forest from about 1120 to the 1370s. This did not mean it was covered in trees, but that special protection was given to deer and other wild animals for hunting. Woe betide you if you stopped the deer getting food by protecting your crops with a fence, or if you failed to cut your dog's claws – they might hurt a boar. And if you were caught poaching, you would probably be blinded or killed. It was tough in those days!

9. At the roundabout, take the second exit, Red Hill Road, back to the start.

Walk 7. Raby

A former racecourse – pretty woodland – fine views – an ancient village

Start and finish: Raby, by the Wheatsheaf Inn

Refreshments: The Wheatsheaf Inn

Distance: Just under 3 miles; allow 1½ hours.

Walking Conditions: Easy walking; flat. May be muddy in places.

This short, simple walk is a bit of a gem. Mostly following little-used paths and tracks, it often has a remote feel and offers a surprising variety of interest.

The starting point, Raby, is mentioned in the Domesday Book of 1086. The village name is Norse for 'village by a boundary' and may indicate that this is the southern limit of an area settled by Norsemen, after they had been driven out of Ireland in the 10th century AD. There are several other Wirral place-names ending in the Norse word 'by' (see photo, opposite).

Sign to a place called 'By' in Sweden. Wirral villages such as Raby got their names form Scandinavian settlers.

The thatched and timber-beamed Wheatsheaf is known to date back to 1611 and may be much older. In 1997 the owner of the adjacent farm, who had developed an allergy to cows, took over the pub and the cowshed was converted into the restaurant!

1. With your back to the pub, go right to Raby Road, then turn left into Raby Mere Road.

   Once, if you had turned right here, the road would have taken you to Raby Mere just over a mile away. The mere is an artificial lake, created as a pond to power a watermill in the early 17th century.

A barn in Raby

Today, though, there is no direct road to the mill – the M53 has blocked it off.

2. 25m after the telephone box go through the wooden gate to the right of the hedge. The gate has a small 'MAFF Conservation Walk' label on it.

The spire of one of All Saints Church at Thornton Hough punctuates the fine views to the right.

3. Keep on the path, running parallel to the road. When the path ends, continue along the verge.

4. Cross the road and go down School Lane.

There was once a viewing stand and horse racecourse to your left along School Lane, one of several racecourses on the Wirral (see also walks 6, 12 and 16). This one was marked on maps in the mid 19th century and the 'School' lane name probably relates to a school for horses or horsemanship.

The track is lined with ash and sycamore trees. Many of the latter

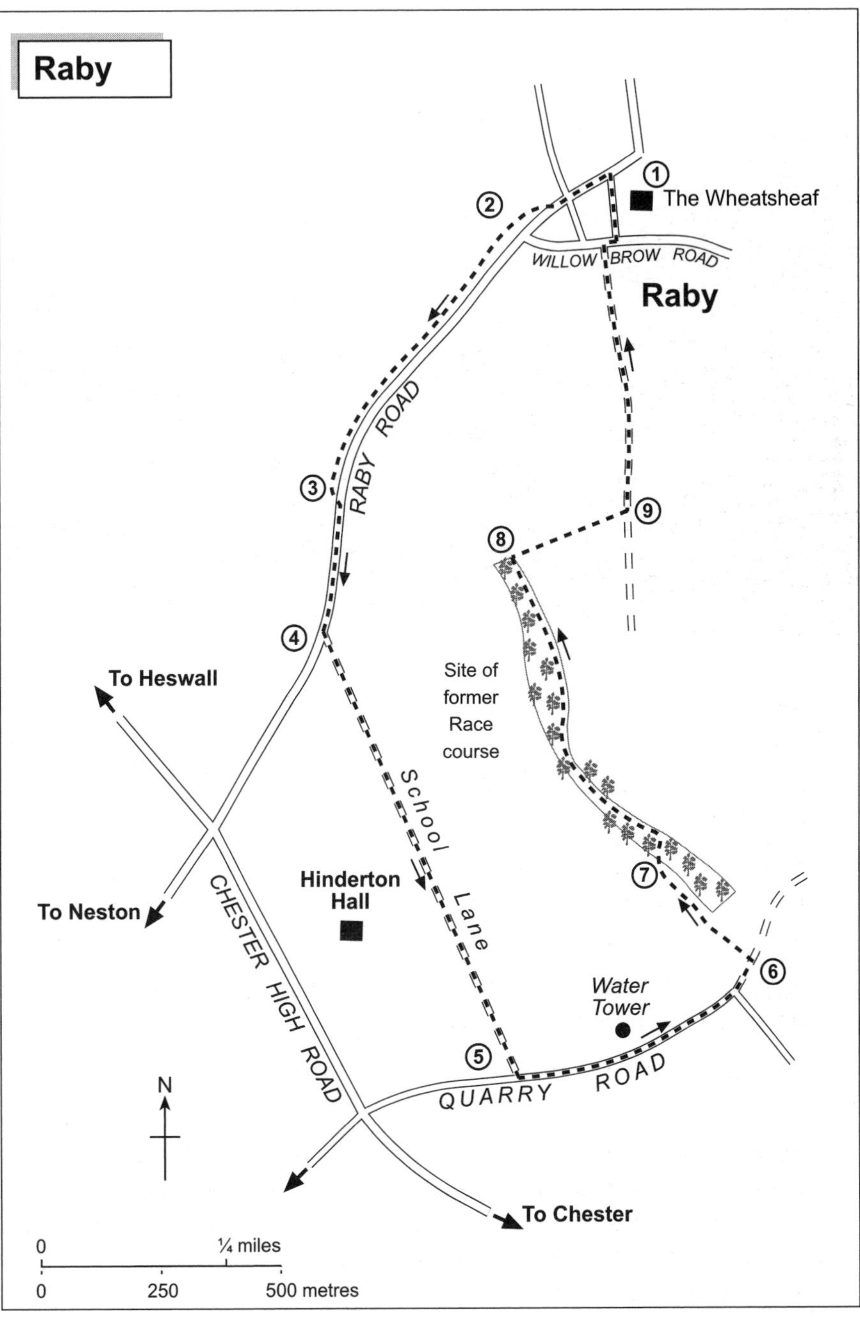
Raby
1
The Wheatsheaf
2
WILLOW BROW ROAD
Raby
RABY ROAD
3
9
8
4
To Heswall
Site of
former
Race
course
School
Lane
7
To Neston
CHESTER HIGH ROAD
Hinderton
Hall
6
Water
Tower
5
QUARRY ROAD
N
To Chester
0
¼ miles
0
250
500 metres

Horses still use the quiet lane by the old racecourse

have been cut back to their base, as if they have been 'coppiced'. Under this ancient practice deciduous trees were cut right back to the stump. This encouraged new growth in the form of several shoots rising from the stump – called a 'coppice stool – to make straight and sturdy poles. These might be used to make fences, or wattle for 'wattle and daub' walls in houses. Another benefit of coppicing is that it greatly prolongs the life of the tree. The sycamores here have been allowed to grow into larger trunks.

Just over halfway along the lane, to your right, you pass a sandstone house. This lodge was built in 1856 – one of three serving Hinderton Hall, visible beyond the lodge, built for a Liverpool wine merchant.

5. At the end of the lane, turn left into Quarry Road.

After about 250m a glance over the fence of 'Theakston', on the right, reveals a quarry, one of three in Quarry Road. The sandstone here was used in road building. There was another quarry on the opposite side of the road. This yielded good building stone, which was used for the large, round water tower you can glimpse from the road. The tower, built in 1884, has been skilfully converted into a five-storey house.

Continue to where the road bends right, crossing very carefully beforehand.

This is true: just round the corner, on the right, once stood a place called 'Sod Hall'. There's nothing there today either!

6. At the bend, go straight ahead into Bluebell Lane. Before reaching 'Rose House' go through a metal kissing gate tucked in the hedge on your left – careful, it is easy to miss. Follow the right-hand field boundary, passing more old quarries to our right.

7. At the end of the field cross a stile to enter a delightful deciduous wood. Keep to the main path.

When the views open up you can see the Liverpool skyline and, 30 miles away to the north-east, Winter Hill topped by its giant TV mast. The top of the mast is 750 metres above sea level.

8. At the T-junction of paths, by stone gateposts, turn right.

9. Cross the stile to the farm track and go left to return to the start.

A question for children: what is odd about the upstairs window of the cottage just before you reach Willowbrow Road?

Walk 8. Thurstaston Common and Royden Park

Views – meadowland – a miniature railway – woodland – Thor's Stone – heathland – Hillbark House

Start and finish: Thurstaston Common car park on the A540, 250m from the Cottage Loaf pub; (or at Royden Park, starting the walk at point 5).

Refreshments: Cottage Loaf pub near Thurstaston car park; Farmer's Arms near entrance to Royden park; teashop may be open at weekends at Royden. Numerous picnic spots.

Distance: 3 miles; allow 2 hours.

Walking Conditions: Mostly easy, dry walking; some uneven ground over rocks near the start.

I always thought that Thurstaston Common was a very popular spot for a stroll. But when I've walked this route – often in perfect walking weather – I've been surprised to go for long stretches without seeing another person, so maybe this lovely walk will be new to you.

It covers the 'Royden Park and Thurstaston Local Nature Reserve'. Royden is an area of open spaces, meres (lakes) and coniferous and deciduous woodland, much of which has developed from old plantations. Thurstaston is a mix of heathland – characterised by heathers, gorse and birch – and woodland, most of which has established itself naturally.

1. From the car park go through the wide gap in the logs by a notice board and climb the sandy path. Continue uphill to the viewpoint.

   There are great views from here – to North Wales (including Anglesey on a clear day); up the Lancashire coast; and across to Liverpool and the Pennines in the distance. The North Hoyle Windfarm is now a distinctive feature off Prestatyn. The 30 turbines, each 40 metres high, generate electricity for up to 50,000 homes.

   Around you is the heathland area of Thurstaston Common.

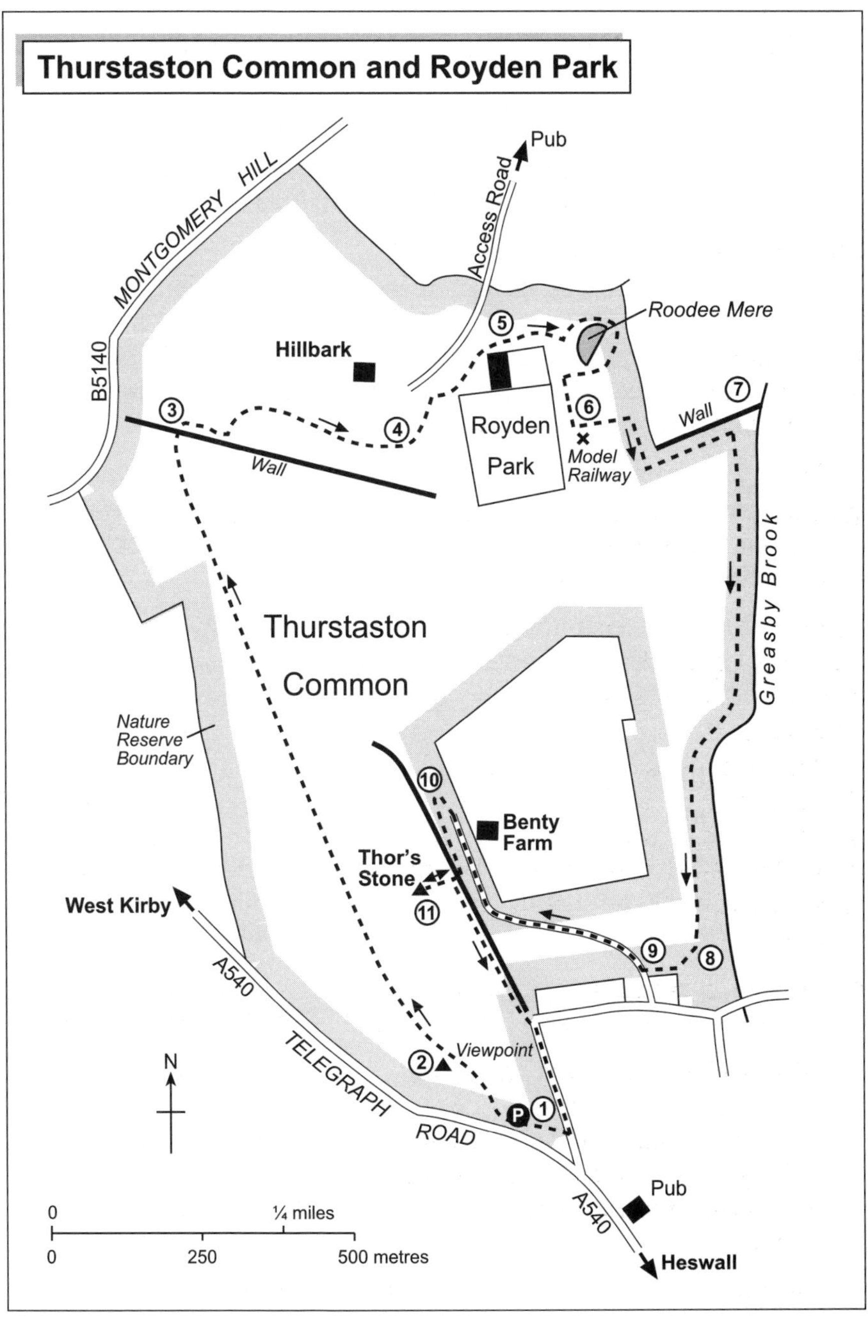
Thurstaston Common and Royden Park
MONTGOMERY HILL
B5140
Access Road
Pub
Hillbark
Royden Park
Roodee Mere
Model Railway
Wall
Wall
Wall
Greasby Brook
Thurstaston Common
Nature Reserve Boundary
Benty Farm
Thor's Stone
West Kirby
A540
TELEGRAPH ROAD
Viewpoint
N
Pub
A540
Heswall
0
¼ miles
0
250
500 metres

Heathland is characterised by poor soils which only a limited range of plants including heathers, gorse and bilberry can tolerate. Birch, oak and rowan also try to get a foothold in the soil. Heathland habitat is under threat across the UK and, as Thurstaston is the largest and best remaining example in Merseyside, it has been designated as a Site of Special Scientific Interest.

The flat-topped concrete structure is a triangulation pillar (often called a 'trig. point'), made as part of a process started in the 1930s to accurately map the whole of the UK. 6173 were built and the job was not finished until 1962. My guess is that this is the most visited trig. point on the Wirral.

2. With your back to the viewpoint, go left, keeping to the main path along the ridge. Stay on this path which gently drops – you should continue to have good views for some time; do not drop onto the lower ground to your left.

Eventually you enter oak and birch woodland, staying on the main path. Continue ahead after the man-made section and eventually reach a wall in front of you.

It is hard to imagine now but the Royden Park area was largely fields until the mid-19th century. The walls formed part of the field boundaries.

3. Go through the gap in the wall and turn right. After about 100 metres, as the path splits near a collapsed section of wall, turn left. Soon reach an open area and turn right, following the main path up the meadow.

Soon Hillbark, a mock-Tudor mansion, comes into view on the left. Extraordinarily, this great house used to sit on Bidston Hill and was moved brick by brick in 1931 to its current position by Sir Ernest Royden, after whom the park is named. It is now run as a hotel but retains extraordinary internal architectural features including a fireplace created by influential 18th century designer Robert Adam; stained-glass windows by the Pre-Raphaelite William Morris (whose designs are still popular in fashion and

The paths around the Common can be surprisingly empty

interior decorating today) and another fireplace once owned by Sir Walter Raleigh.

In summer the meadow is full of flowers, including birdsfoot trefoil with its curved yellow petals; and common spotted orchid with pink flowers and leaves marked with dark spots. The meadow attracts many butterflies.

4. At the top of the meadow, fork left of the metal bench and go straight ahead, up a short hill, alongside a wooden fence. At the top of the hill turn left and take a clear path across a small open area and though rhododendron bushes.

At some brown posts (without a gate) turn right to the car park. Make your way through the car park, bearing slightly left to reach buildings.

5. Walk to the left of the buildings and high wall, past a green metal gate, signed to 'Roodee Mere'.

Stop off at the Walled Nature Garden, managed through the

Working on a model steam train at Royden Park

Royden Park Project, a horticulture and woodwork employment training project for adults with learning difficulties, run by Wirral Social Services. There is much to look at including a wildlife pond, herb garden and several sculptures.

Continue down the track to bend right and cross the miniature railway line. Go clockwise round Roodee Mere.

The railway is usually open on summer Sunday afternoons and on Bank Holiday Mondays. Admire the working scale model engines – or join the nearby queue to ride one!

6. On reaching the rail line again, go left for 75 metres and then take a left turn at the fence, signed to Thurstaston Wood. Follow the main path, which bends right after 100 metres or so. 50 metres later look for a stone wall starting on your left. Turn left and walk with the wall on your left for about 200 metres.

7. At the bottom of the hill do not cross the footbridge, but go right and follow the path beside Greasby Brook through woodland filled with the sweet scent of Scots pine.

At a cross-paths, take the narrow path immediately left of a large wooden bench, soon turning right onto a wider path. Go through the gate at a wire fence and continue ahead.

8. Go though the gate at a second fence and immediately turn right along a path, over fallen trees.

Soon, at a field corner, turn right and go through a gate fitted with an ingenious lifting mechanism! Soon reach a track.

9. Go straight ahead, and stay on the track for about 400 metres to pass Benty Farm.

There are several 'Benty' names on the Wirral. They probably come from 'Bent hay', bent being a kind of hay grass. Bent is also a medieval word for an unenclosed pasture or heath.

10. Shortly after the farm, the track narrows – a few metres later double back, down the narrow path across marshy ground. Go though a gate in the wall and straight ahead for 50 metres to reach Thor's Stone.

There are many theories about the origins of this huge rock with its extraordinary curved gullies – most dramatically that it was a place of worship and sacrifice for Viking settlers. The truth is probably more mundane: it is more likely to have been the mount for a crane in an old sandstone quarry.

11. Retrace your steps and turn right immediately before the wall. Continue ahead to reach the road and go straight on, along a man-made path. About 50 metres after school buildings look for any of the clear paths on the right, back to the car park.

Walk 9. Eastham Country Park

Woodland – river views – sea-life sculptures – a former pleasure gardens and zoo – Mersey ferry crossings

Start and finish: Eastham Country Park car park, signposted from the A41.

Distance: 3¼ miles; allow 2 hours (but can be shortened by cutting out the loops at points 2 and 5)

Refreshments: pubs and tea garden near the car park.

Walking Conditions: fairly level; mostly good paths suitable for cycles and pushchairs (with many alternative paths available).

This walk combines great views up and down the Mersey, the variety and beauty of the woodlands at Eastham, and evidence of the area's varied history. A Visitor Centre, and a noticeboard opposite The Tap pub, give much interesting information.

Eastham was an important crossing point between Liverpool and the Wirral for centuries. Its popularity waned when the railway opened between Birkenhead and Liverpool 1846, but the area was revived with the addition of the Eastham Ferry Hotel and Pleasure Gardens. These were a huge attraction for decades but declined in the 1920s. The last ferry – a paddle steamer – left in 1929.

1. From the car park drop down the hill and turn right. Opposite The Tap is a jetty, built in the 1870s to serve the Mersey ferry. The bay-fronted sandstone building nearby was the ticket office.

Notice also the superb Marine Life sculptures nearby, celebrating the variety of sea creatures found around Wirral's coast. There are also decorative tiles made by local school children.

2. Walk along the promenade:

This gives views towards the entrance to the Manchester Ship Canal, opened in 1894 by Queen Victoria. The 35-mile canal linked Manchester with the sea for the benefit of traders, particularly cotton importers and textile exporters. It attracted

Job's Ferry: Ships have been using the Mersey here for hundreds of years

millions of sightseers during its construction. Return by the same route (or scramble up the steep bank and turn right).

3. Retrace your steps to the mini-roundabout, then walk along the riverside road which becomes a path.

4. Look for a gate in the metal fencing to your right.

This leads to Jobs Ferry, now just a collection of scattered sandstone blocks. This was the original site of the ferry station to cross the Mersey, which is believed to have operated since the 13th century, initially by monks. The green and red buoys in the river are used to guide ships using the canal.

5. Continue on the path to a fence of metal railings, marking the boundary of the Park. For excellent views, continue alongside the river for 350m keeping to the main path.

The raised grassy area to your left was once the site of the coal-fired Bromborough Power Station, now demolished. The large concrete quay next to the river was the unloading area for ships bringing coal.

There are fine views of the Mersey. Liverpool is to the left, the airport to your half-right. In the distance, up the Mersey, on a clear day you can make out the Runcorn Bridge 10 miles away.

Return along the top of the grassy bank, accessible on your left shortly after the path bends away from the river.

Several rail lines to the power station once ran along this bank, part of an extensive rail network serving local industry, built from 1910 but now vanished.

6. Back at the metal fence, turn right and follow a variable path running roughly parallel with the fence.

The gentle hill you walk over is not natural. There used to be a sandstone quarry here, which was infilled with rubble from the demolition of the power station. The rubble was piled higher than the natural ground level, making an artificial hill.

After about 125 metres the metal fence to your right turns into one made of wooden stakes. 10m later take a path to the left walking past a long line of poplars.

The sycamores on the right have been felled as they were crowding out other plants, and were damaging the bank which is retaining industrial waste.

7. At a meeting of paths, fork right.

There are concrete blocks each side of the path at the junction. These used to carry an overhead steam pipe from the power station.

After 150 metres meet a wide path (with remains of a wall 20m to your right) and go straight across it – i.e. do not take the path past the wall.

8. Shortly after, reach a massive beech tree which children can climb inside.

Beech and oak are the dominant trees in the woodland. This beech used to be the tallest tree on Wirral (at least 28 metres high) until 2003 when part of it came down in a storm and much of the rest had to be cut back. It is thought to be over 300 years old. The felled wood was used to make the marine life sculptures near the jetty.

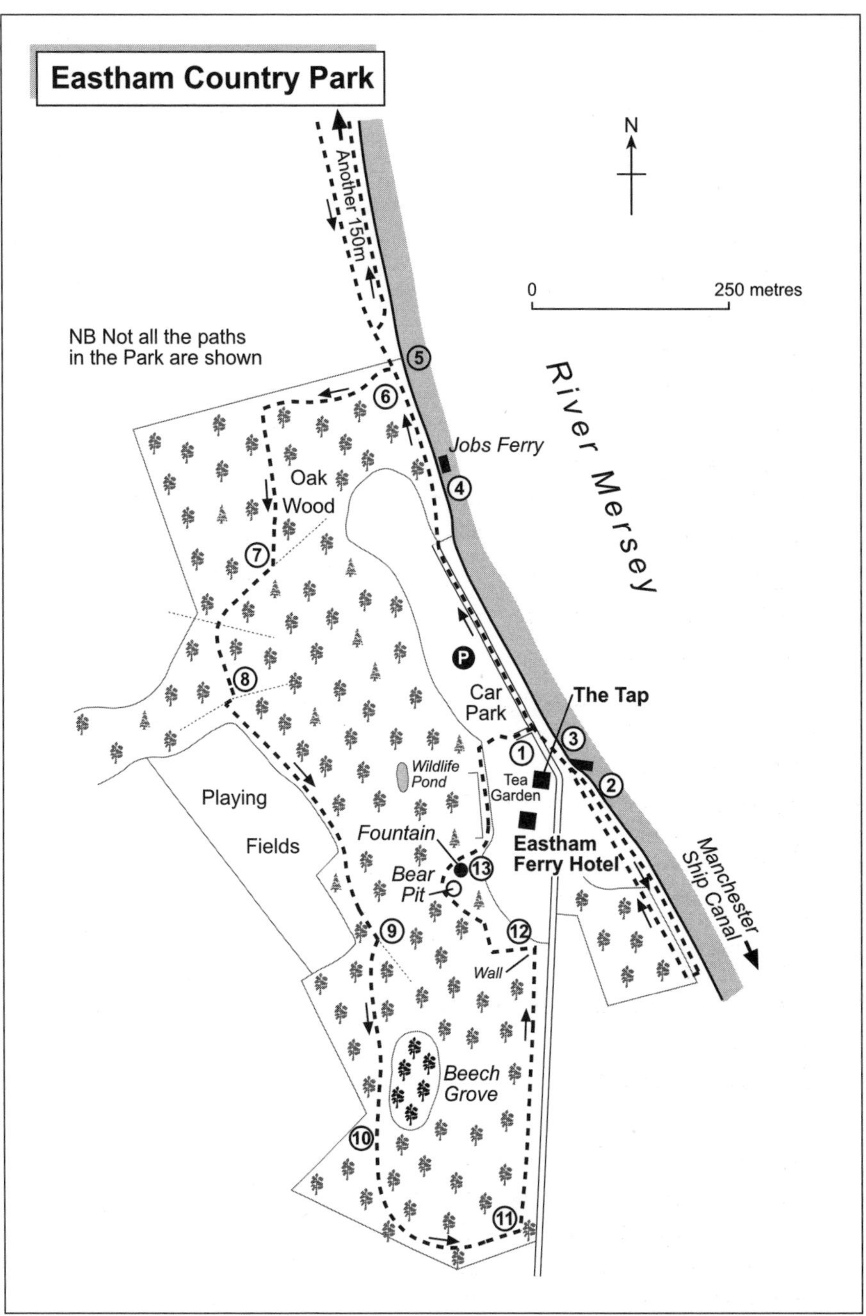
Eastham Country Park
Another 150m
N
0
250 metres
NB Not all the paths in the Park are shown
River Mersey
Jobs Ferry
Oak Wood
Car Park
The Tap
Tea Garden
Wildlife Pond
Playing
Fields
Fountain
Bear Pit
Eastham Ferry Hotel
Manchester Ship Canal
Wall
Beech Grove

Marine life carvings made from the ancient beech tree on the route

Turn right for a few metres, then take a path left, just before playing fields, and keep on it, ignoring paths to left.

You may notice bird-boxes along here and elsewhere in the wood. Some are for tawny and short-eared owls; others for tits. The boxes with no hole at the front are for bats, which enter through a slit underneath.

9. Keep an eye open for a gap in the trees to your right as you pass a corner of the playing fields; take the next main path you come to on the right, about 120 metres after this gap. There is an oak tree in front of you at this fork.

After 250 metres Beech Grove, to your left as you near a wall, is a magnificent stand of mature beeches. It is also known as 'The Cathedral' – when the trees are in leaf the canopy forms a great cathedral-like ceiling, with scattered shafts of sunlight as if coming through the windows.

10. Continue on the path, which soon curves left.

You pass several conifers with delicate, flat needles – these are Western hemlocks.

11. Stay on the path as it bends left by a gate to the road and then widens. Eventually reach the remains of a sandstone wall.

The wall marks the edge of the old Pleasure Gardens. This area comprised magnificent gardens and many other attractions: a zoo with lions, leopards, camels, monkeys and more; entertainments including a ballroom, bandstand and stage; and fairground attractions including a water chute and loop-the-loop roller coaster, thought to be the first in the country. There are good pictures of the Gardens in the Visitor Centre.

12. Follow the wall left for 40m to reach two low sandstone pillars. Turn right, towards a conifer, and take the path forking left just before this tree. Shortly, when you reach jagged rocks ahead of you, fork left, reaching the circular Bear Pit 50 metres later.

Continue on the main path and soon reach one of two sandstone fountains in the Gardens. Notice also a man-made 'cave' on the left – either for the water pump, or to house more animals.

13. Drop down the steps and take the next path left to walk alongside the wall of the former boating lake. This takes you back to the start.

Take a moment to look at the huge oak tree at the top of the children's play area next to the car park (one of its fallen branches has been carved into a dragon). This has been dated to at least 500 years old – before Henry VIII came to the throne.

Walk 10. Brimstage and Thornton Hough

Farm-pet animals – craft centre – wildlife – an environmentally friendly farm estate – historic villages

Start and finish: Brimstage Hall Courtyard, 1 mile from the Clatterbridge roundabout on the A5137.

Distance: 3½ miles; allow 2 hours, plus stopping time at Brimstage and Thornton Hough.

Refreshments: The Seven Stars pub in Thornton Hough; tea and coffee shops in both villages.

Walking conditions: generally good, but parts can be quite muddy when wet.

Most of this walk is across attractive land which has been managed as a showpiece environmentally friendly farm. It also takes in the attractive villages of Brimstage and Thornton Hough, each with very different histories.

Start with a look around the Brimstage Hall development: the craft shops are great places for gift ideas. And the Family Farm is a 'must' for children where they can see, and maybe feed or stroke, a variety of animals including llamas, goats, rabbits, a highland cow and a pot-bellied pig. It is open every day and the admission fee includes a pot of food for the animals.

From the courtyard you can see the top of the three-storey tower at the back of Brimstage Hall. It's probably 700-800 years old and may have been a pele tower – a rectangular, fortified residence more usually found in the Scottish borders. The tower has 'machicolations' – overhanging holes at the top from which things could be dropped on attackers – and arrow slits. The Hall also once had a moat – though in medieval times moats were more often status symbols than needed for defence.

1. Walk down the entrance driveway. Turn right, walking along the road for about 200m.

Brimstage Hall

Large village greens are unusual in Cheshire (historically, this is Cheshire) – this one was created in 1913. On the far side is a white barn bearing a datestone of 1758.

2. Take the footpath signposted right to Thornton Hough, using sandstone steps. Follow this path straight head and cross a farm track, via two stiles.

The field immediately after the sandstone steps is very bumpy. I've always wondered why, but one possibility is that it was an old quarry which has been filled in with rubble – Brimstage sits on sandstone which is just below the surface; this stone would have been easily accessible for building walls and buildings.

3. Bear slightly left, then over another stile and walk to the right of a hedge.

The hawthorn hedge was being 'laid' in early 2005. The stems are virtually cut through and then bent almost to ninety degrees. This encourages strong new growth, thickening the hedge and

Hedge laying on the Leverhulme Estate

prolonging its life, as well as making a more attractive habitat for wildlife.

Near the far-right-hand corner of the field, you can see a box on top of a pole. This is for barn owls to nest in.

At a field junction the path moves to the left of a hedge, but keeps in the same direction.

Keep your eyes open for a variety of wildlife including buzzards wheeling, kestrels hovering, pheasants and partridges. I have seen several brown hares at close-quarters along this stretch.

4. Cross a tree-lined track via two more stiles, and straight cross a field to reach a T-junction of paths. Turn left along a sunken path to meet an estate track.

This impressive avenue, and others including the well-known Lever Causeway at Storeton, were built by the first Viscount Leverhulme (who also built the attractive estates in Port Sunlight and Thornton Hough). He planned to put residential housing along them, and allowed space for a central road and an outer service road on each side. But with the outbreak of the First World War, his plan was never fulfilled.

5. Ignore tracks to left and right; instead continue straight over the junction, passing to the left of some low conifers, onto a track that soon bends right (ignore the track that forks to the left on the bend).

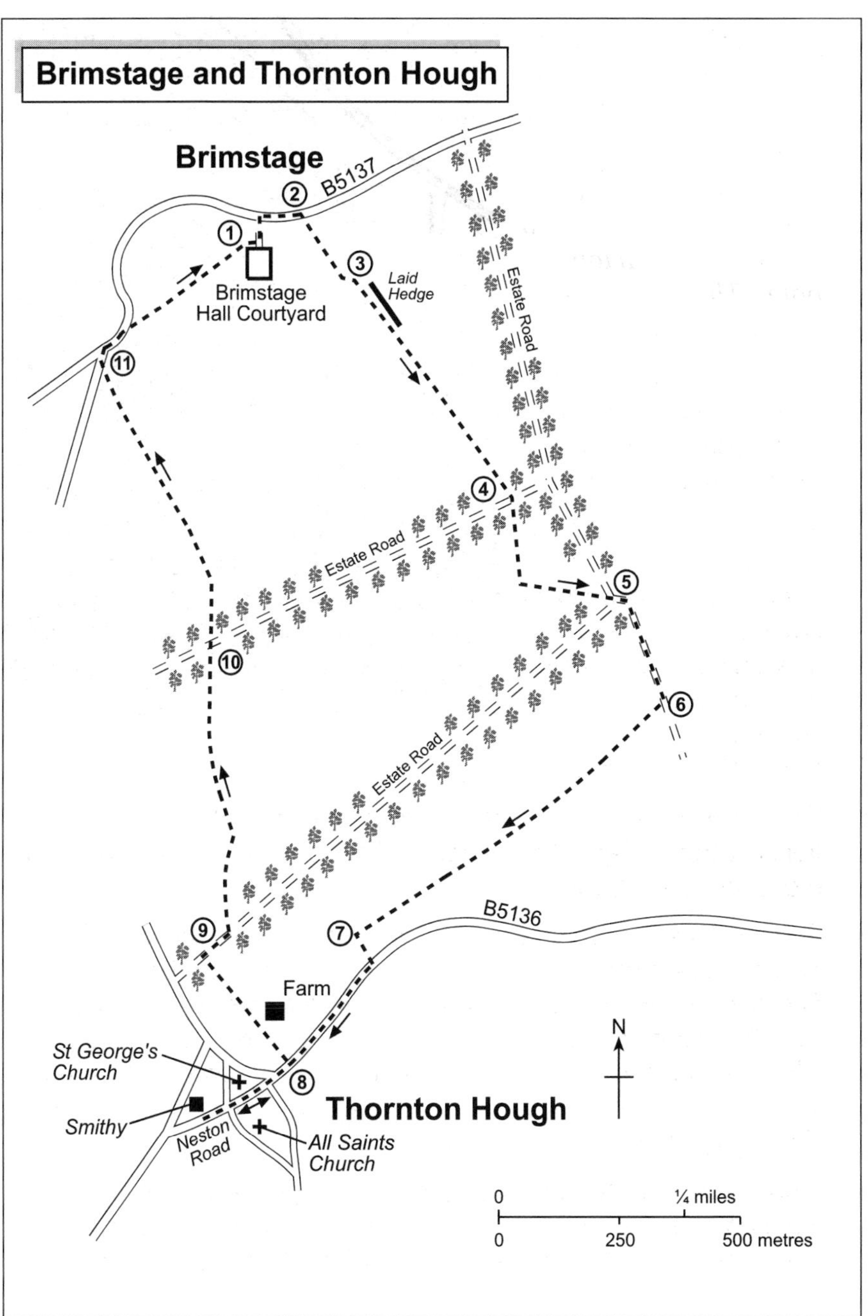
Brimstage and Thornton Hough
Brimstage
B5137
Brimstage Hall Courtyard
Laid Hedge
Estate Road
Estate Road
Estate Road
B5136
Farm
St George's Church
Smithy
Neston Road
All Saints Church
Thornton Hough
N
0
¼ miles
0
250
500 metres

6. After about 220 metres pass a metal gate and 20 metres later, at another metal gate, turn right over a stile, to walk alongside a hedge. Meet and follow a line of telegraph poles and stay on this heading to reach a track.

7. Turn left to meet the B5136. Cross to the pavement and turn right to walk into Thornton Hough.

Thornton Hough is an ancient settlement, mentioned in the 1086 Domesday Book. However the village we see today is the product of two successful businessmen – The Victorian Joseph Hirst, a Yorkshire woollen manufacturer and William Lever (later Viscount Leverhulme) who established the successful soap factory at Port Sunlight in 1888.

The village has two large churches – the Parish church with the tall spire built by Hirst, and St George's Church, with its squat tower, by Lever. (Lever did not want the church to dominate the village so, as well as having a low tower, he lowered the ground the church was on by over a metre). From the top of the village, you will notice the Parish church has five clocks – Hirst added the extra one, as the roof of the church did not allow him to see the clock from his bedroom window.

Look at the weather vane on Lever's church – a cockerel and bugle. This is a visual pun on his name: 'lever' in French means 'to get up', and the cock and the bugle are both forms of early morning wake-up calls!

Hirst built several buildings at the upper end of the village – you can see his initials on The Turret. But Lever was responsible for the rest, most of which were to house his estate workers.

There is an extraordinary mix of architecture here: sometimes you can see black and white carved timbers, elsewhere brick or sandstone block. Roofs are made from thatch, slate and coloured tile, and even the chimneystacks are elaborate. Take a look at the first few houses on Neston Road to see ornately carved woodwork (above the windows and on the gable of no. 1); pargetting (decorative plasterwork, on no. 2 above the windows); stone carving, and ornamental ironwork on doors and windows (on nos.

3 & 4). It's also worth looking at the picturesque smithy at the bottom of the hill, especially if it's operating.

8. After looking around retrace your steps and take the path signed 'Public Footpath to Brimstage' near the red telephone box.

The Leverhulme Farm on your right was, until recently, a member of the LEAF (Linking the Environment and Farming) scheme, actively managing the land in an environmentally friendly way. At the time of writing, a change in management is underway but it is hoped that this approach to conservation will continue. Wildlife is encouraged, for example by providing the boxes for barn owls and tree sparrows, and leaving wide unploughed margins at the edge of arable fields for animals to hide in. New hedges and trees are planted; animals are reared humanely; and the use of chemicals is extremely carefully controlled.

9. After 250m, reach an estate road. Turn right for 50m, then left down a clear path signed to Brimstage. Continue on this path crossing two stiles – the first made from a slab of sandstone; the second is more conventional and gives a good view of Thornton Manor gatehouse to your half-left. Continue on the clear path, passing a small stand of Scots pine with their characteristic bare lower trunks.

10. Cross another estate road, lined with sycamores, via two kissing gates. Then bear slightly right to reach another sandstone slab stile. Cross and continue ahead, to reach a further stile and, a few metres later, a path junction. Continue straight ahead. After 500 metres you will come to a road.

On your right, you will see a large area of deciduous saplings, planted in 2004 as part of the Leverhulme Estate's stewardship scheme for the land.

11. Turn right for 150m. When the road bends left, take a stile by the black and white traffic chevrons to cross the field back to Brimstage Hall.

Walk 11. Frankby and Larton

Parkland and farmland – giraffe food – a former RAF camp – a tree plantation – old farming methods – traditional buildings

Start and finish: Royden Park car park, off the B5140.

Distance: 3½ or 3¾ miles; allow 2 hours.

Refreshments: picnic sites, and teashop occasionally open, at Royden Park; Farmer's Arms pub at Frankby.

Walking Conditions: flat with some gentle slopes; often good tracks and paths, but the sections across fields can be very muddy.

This is a varied walk through woodland, farmland and an unusual plantation. Many of the paths are little used so the route often feels remote despite being near built-up areas. There are magnificent old buildings around point 6 and at Frankby, worth taking time to admire.

Royden Park was farmland until the mid 19th century. Now, attractions include a walled nature garden, and model railways offering rides on Sundays and bank holidays, subject to the weather.

1. At the four-way crossing just before the car park, take the track signed to Frankby Mere and Montgomery Hill.

2. After 250m, opposite a gate, take a path left to make a clockwise circuit of Frankby Mere (in summer you will probably find it has dried out). This is a pleasant detour through Corsican and Scots pine, birch and rhododendrons. A path to the left, shortly after the bird-hide on the right, leads to a pretty, open area ideal for picnics.

   You will notice that some of the trees in the mere have been severely cut back. These are willows, which are coppiced every four years (for more on 'coppicing' see page 38) by the team at the Royden Park Project, which provides employment training for adults with learning difficulties. The cut branches are sent to feed the giraffes at Chester Zoo.

3. Back on the track, continue to a road. Cross and go right for 100m.

Giraffes at Chester Zoo, happy consumers of foliage from Royden Park (photo: Chester Zoo)

Turn left between walls, by the 'Birch Hey, Private Road' sign, and immediately right, signed to Grange.

Notice how the fields to your left are long and quite narrow. They grew out of the 'old ridge and furrow' farming system used in the middle ages. Land for farming was not split into fields surrounded by the hedges we take for granted in the countryside today. Instead land was divided into long thin strips which were banked up to form 'ridges' a few metres wide, with shallow ditches – 'furrows' – in between. The whole of the arable land would be divided into these strips, large groups of which formed 'open fields'. The strips were allocated to the people who lived in the village to grow their crops on. This allocation was often apparently haphazard so that someone might own one strip in one place and another one 100 metres away – it was a very inefficient way of farming. Later the pattern of the long strips was used as the basis for laying out the fields we see today.

4. Straight over the road and down "Frankby Stiles" towards the riding complex at Larton, passing landscaped fishing ponds. Do not take the turning for the farm, but continue straight ahead along the rough track after the yellow 'Only Food for Horses' Reliant Robin. At a T-junction of paths turn left and soon cross a concrete bridge

5. Follow the field boundary on your left to reach a stile. Cross it and aim diagonally right, to the field corner, just left of a house.

You are walking over a series of ridges about 15m wide. These, again, are the remains of the "ridge and furrow" farming system. One advantage of this system is that the furrows improved drainage of the sticky clay soil.

6. Cross the stile and turn right, later following the road round the corner.

China Farm, is named after a plate made of china set into the farmhouse wall. The farm was built in the 1700s by a former Mayor of Liverpool. At China Farm, notice the large entrance to the long brick barn, and a similar doorway on the far side. These used to help farmers with "winnowing" – separating the grain they had harvested from its husk, the chaff. When the two parts were separated inside the barn, the draft through the doors (which face the prevailing wind) blew the lighter chaff away. The triangular sections sticking out from each side of the entrance supported the open doors, which funnelled the wind through the barn.

7. Opposite a modern bungalow (Newton Hall Cottage) cross the stile; over a track and continue over two more stiles. With the pond on your left, follow the hedge to a fourth stile.

8. From the stile, continue on the same heading, towards the left-hand side of trees visible over the brow of the hill, across the field and passing over a track.

9. Cross a stile and continue ahead to a concrete path. Turn right, signed "Frankby".

The tracks are part of the site of former RAF West Kirby, the buildings and roads of which were laid out in a grid system. No aircraft were ever based here; instead, it was used as a WWII transit camp for British airmen waiting to go overseas, and airmen from allied countries who came here to fight. After the war, it became a "boot camp" for men doing National Service.

10. Go through two gates and under power lines after which the track narrows. When the metalled track bends right, fork left down a narrow path to cross a wooden footbridge.

11. Keep the field boundary to your left, to reach two stiles and a track.

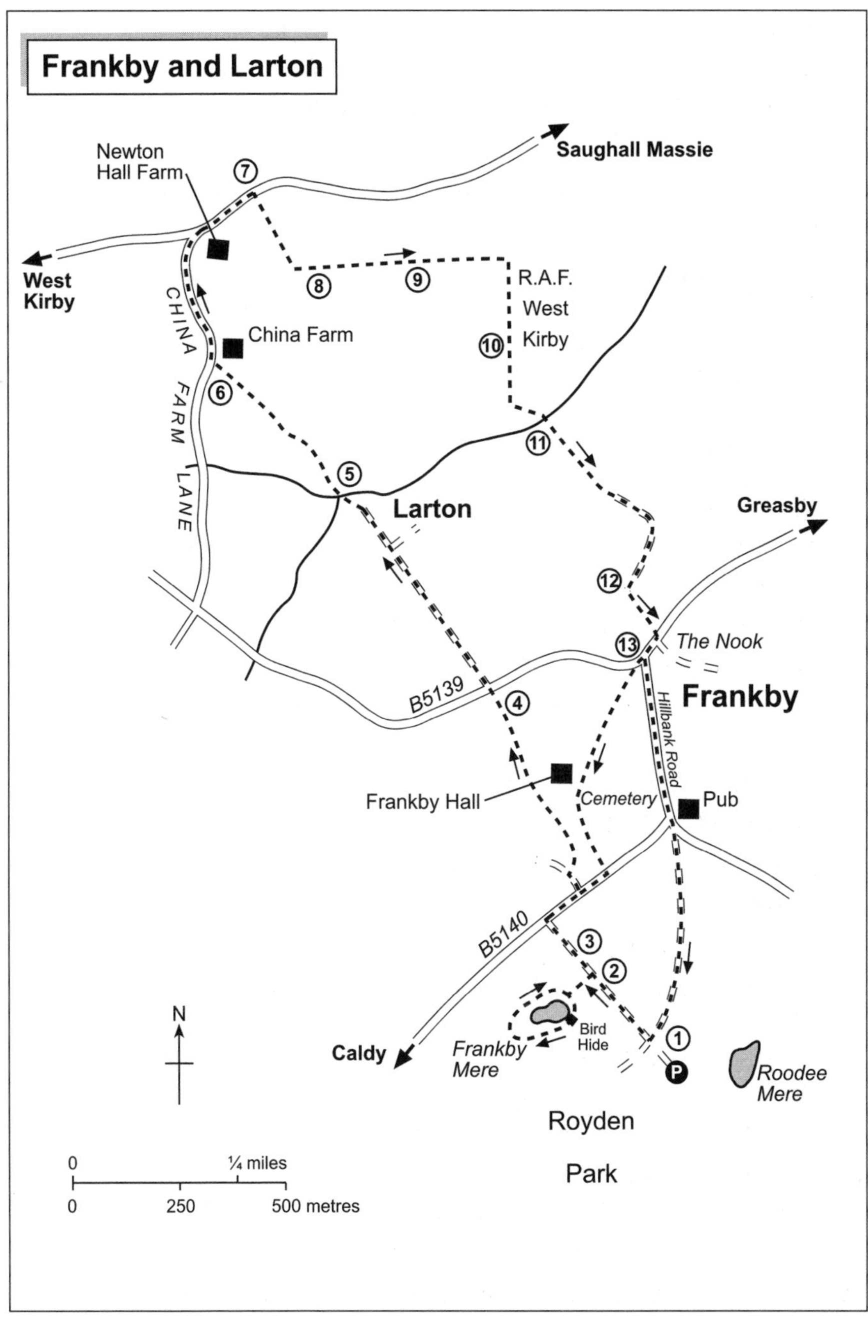
Frankby and Larton
Saughall Massie
Newton Hall Farm
West Kirby
China Farm
CHINA FARM LANE
R.A.F. West Kirby
Larton
Greasby
The Nook
Frankby
Hillbank Road
B5139
Frankby Hall
Cemetery
Pub
B5140
Caldy
Bird Hide
Frankby Mere
Roodee Mere
Royden Park
N
0 ¼ miles
0 250 500 metres

RAF West Kirby in 1947 *(Photo credit: see Preface)*

12. At stables, look for a footpath sign "To Frankby" (note further obvious 'ridges' in the field to your right). Turn right at the road.

Frankby and West Kirby both have 'by' name endings, indicating they were settled by Norsemen who came to the Wirral just after AD900 (see photo, p.41). Similarly, the first part of the name 'Larton' comes from 'leirr', an Old Norse word for clay.

There are many lovely old buildings clustered around and near Frankby's small village green. This is a Conservation Area and the buildings are mostly made of traditional materials: sandstone, hand-made brick and slate roofs. Many have datestones from the 1700s, and Half Inn House, up 'The Nook' (leading off the green), says '1675'.

13. At the junction, you have a choice. Either

a) Go left, up Hillbark Road, for a slightly shorter route and to pass the pub; continue up the road to the entrance to the park. Cross and continue up the access road; or

b) To take in the peace of Frankby Cemetery, and to admire Sir

Frankby Hall with its castle-like features

Thomas Royden's castle-like house, cross the road and enter the cemetery between the stone gateposts. Continue ahead, to the house.

The cemetery land used to be owned by Royden, the grandfather of Ernest whom the park is named after. Sir Thomas was a shipbuilding millionaire, and the cemetery's chapel and administration HQ were once his grand home, Frankby Hall. He built it in 1847 in the fashionable 19th style – like a castle, with turrets, crenellations (battlements), solid buttresses (wall supports) and even mock arrow-slits.

Take the path left immediately after the building to reach the road. Retrace your steps to the start.

Walk 12. Parkgate

A former ferry and fishing port, and seaside resort – disused railways – coastal walking – saltmarsh – wildlife – great views

Start and finish: Near the Post Office along The Parade.

Distance: 3½ or 5¼ miles; allow 2 or 3 hours

Refreshments: a café and several pubs in Parkgate. Point 12 is a lovely picnic spot.

Walking Conditions: mostly flat; two climbs (one very short). Occasional mud, especially between 9 and 13, but a shorter alternative is available.

The open views of Parkgate are refreshing at any time. But the area can be particularly spectacular during the highest tides when water laps the Parade. The marsh is part of the Gayton Sands reserve owned by the Royal Society for the Protection of Birds. At high tides, the mass of birds is particularly noisy and spectacular, including short-eared owls and sparrowhawks. Call Wirral Country Park Visitor Centre (0151-648-4371) for tide times and natural history information.

Though it is hard to imagine now, Parkgate was once a major port. Where you see the marsh, many-masted sailing ships once floated, often travelling between here and Ireland. The River Dee originally ran all the way along this side of the estuary from Chester but, due to silting, was diverted via the Welsh side in 1737 for some of its length. However, the silting continued and the river eventually became too shallow for ships to moor locally – the last one left in the 1820s.

1. Walk along The Parade past the Boathouse pub, eventually reaching a kissing gate.

As you wander along the Parade keep an eye open for tall grey herons standing on, or flying over, the marsh; you may also see little egrets – smaller, upstanding bright white birds that were very rare until recently.

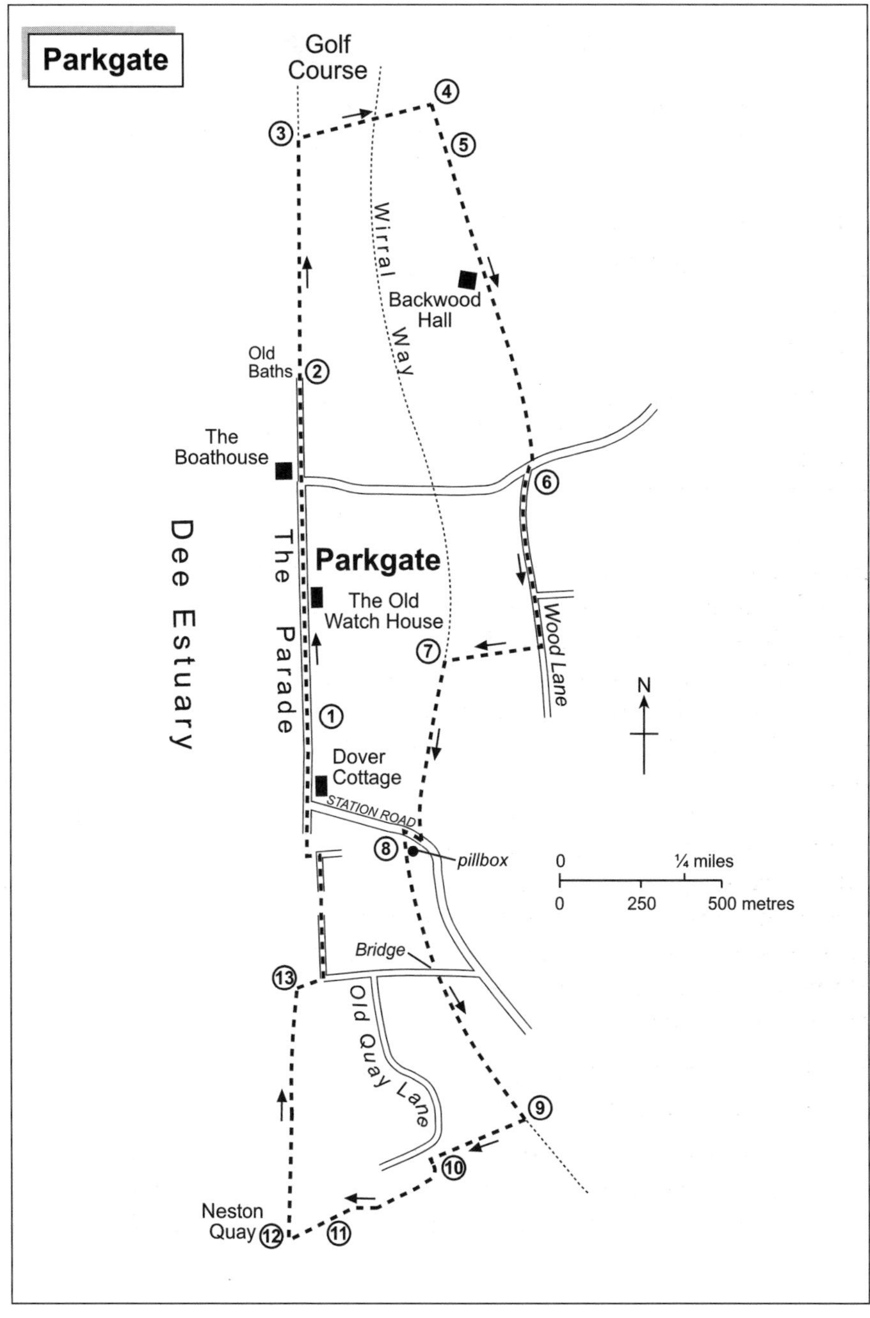
Parkgate
Golf Course
Wirral Way
Backwood Hall
Old Baths
The Boathouse
Dee Estuary
The Parade
Parkgate
The Old Watch House
Wood Lane
Dover Cottage
STATION ROAD
pillbox
N
0 ¼ miles
0 250 500 metres
Bridge
Old Quay Lane
Neston Quay

About 400 metres/¼ mile from the start, where the road temporarily narrows, you will see a sloping slipway down to the marsh. Fishing was an important industry here, especially when Parkgate was no longer a major seaport. Fishing boats moored right against the slipways to bring their catches ashore – the shore was several feet lower than today. There is another slipway just before the Boathouse pub.

The house where the road narrows, The Old Watch House, is where the Customs Officers lived who monitored Parkgate's international trade from the 17th to the 19th centuries.

The grey walls before the gate are the remains of a large seawater swimming pool opened in the 1920s. The owner once wrote a fake complaint letter to a newspaper about the "indecent" swimsuits on show. This pulled in more custom!

2. Follow the sea wall for 500 metres. At a sandstone pillar and wooden bench turn right.

3. Cross the golf course with care, between the blue poles. Go over the Wirral Way and continue to the top of the hill (If you want to avoid a possibly muddy stretch turn right along the Wirral Way and rejoin at point 7).Take in the magnificent views while you get your breath back!

4. Follow the hedge right, to a gate.

5. Continue in the same direction across a field, down a dip, through gates and up the hill. Go along the track.

6. Cross into Wood Lane. After 600 metres take a path on the right, signposted to Parkgate. Parkgate is named after a deer park established about 750 years ago. The path you are on is thought to be the northern boundary of the park.

7. Veer right just before the bridge, then left and over it. Continue on the Wirral Way to Station Road. Turn right.

The Wirral Way is a disused railway track. When the line was first opened in 1866 Parkgate Station was situated on the far side of Station Road. From here, you could catch the train to Hooton,

Parkgate saltmarsh and village

linking with the main Birkenhead to Chester railway line. The line was popular with Victorian day-trippers who could now reach the seaside easily; it also gave easy access to more distant markets for Parkgate's fishermen. In 1886, the railway line was extended to West Kirby and the station moved to the other side of the road, where you have just walked. The south side became sidings, and handled the wagons coming to and from Ness Colliery (Walk 22).

The field visible through the trees on your left shortly before the road – Parksfield – was a popular venue for horse racing in the 19th century.

8. For the short cut, continue down to The Parade (see the note after point 13 below). Otherwise, go left through the kissing gate, by the World War II pillbox, and up the steps.

Go past a gate to rejoin the Wirral Way. Walk under a bridge, still stained with soot from the steam trains.

About 125 metres later, where the good path swings left, a small embankment starts and a hedge forks off to the right. This was the line of a branch railway that ran down to Ness Colliery at Little Neston.

9. About 1km (0.6 miles) from Station Road, at a new fence, go right through a wooden kissing gate. Follow the path to a metal gate.

At the bottom of the first field, by a telegraph pole, the route is crossed by parallel hedges. Again, this is the line of the old railway to the colliery.

10. Turn left for 40m, then right to cross a field. The direct path across the field is often waterlogged. You are best off walking to the left, alongside the stream. At the end of the field cross a footbridge and continue, keeping the hedge to your left.

11. As the path bends left, about 120m before the fence just visible at the marsh edge, fork slightly right to an old sandstone step-stile near trees.

This point is Neston Quay. Now dismantled, the quay was a stone structure jutting into the Dee which, at that time, ran alongside the Wirral shore. It was built in the 17th century as a mooring place for ships trading with Chester, which had silted up. You can still see the brick remains of a building serving the port a few metres before the step-stile, on your left.

12. Turn right and follow the path, crossing a footbridge and later a stile, to walk alongside the marsh.

Soon after the stile you pass reed mace (or bulrushes) with their female flower heads looking like brown sausages. Soon after, you pass huge stands of common reed, which shimmer in the light and rustle in the breeze. The tough stems of reeds like this make them valuable for thatching roofs.

13. After 700m the path detours inland along a road. After a further 450m, at a right-hand bend, pick up the narrow path on your left to take you back to The Parade.

Parkgate had several famous visitors. In 1784, Emma Hamilton, who was born at nearby Ness and who became the mistress of

Walkers on the sea wall at Parkgate

Admiral Lord Nelson, came here to treat a skin complaint by bathing in the waters. Parkgate had been a popular sea-bathing resort since the 1700s, when the golden sands were several feet below the present marsh. Emma stayed at Dover Cottage, the last terraced cottage before the right-hand bend. Other visitors to Parkgate included the composer, Handel, who travelled here from Ireland, and John Wesley, the founder of Methodism, who preached nearby.

Finally, when you have finished the walk, it's time to treat yourself to a famous Parkgate ice cream!

Walk 13. Thurstaston and Wirral Country Park

A waterfall – beach walking – wildlife – the Wirral Way – Ice Age cliffs – a rail accident

Start and finish: Wirral Country Park Visitor Centre at Thurstaston, signposted off the A540 between Heswall and West Kirby.

Distance: 3¾ miles; allow at least 2 hours

Refreshments: café at car park entrance; kiosk at the Visitor Centre. The Cottage Loaf pub is about 300 metres off the route – walk right, up the 'No Entry' road, in Thurstaston village.

Walking Conditions: beach; good paths (some of which may be muddy after rain); one steep but very short climb. Occasionally the route along the beach can become inaccessible because of the tide. Check at the Visitor's Centre before you start.

This is a walk with plenty of contrast – a beach, secluded woodland, high ground with great views, and Wirrals' only natural waterfall. Allow some time at the Visitor Centre. There's a good exhibition, helpful staff, and details of many activities for all ages. There is also a bird hide with plenty of information on what to look out for.

1. Walk across the grass in front of the Centre to the cliff top.

   The humps in the grass are World War II gun emplacements which have been buried rather than demolished. Kite flying is popular here and you may see hang-gliders launching off the cliffs. In front of you lie the Dee Estuary and the coast of north Wales.

   The North Hoyle windfarm is now a distinctive feature off the north Wales coast, near Prestatyn. The 30 turbines, each 40 metres high, generate electricity for up to 50,000 homes.

   Below, you can see small islands of grass in the mud. This is cord-grass, sometimes known by its scientific name of 'Spartina maritima'. Cord-grass has a great ability to trap grains of mud and stop the flow of water. This means that mud gradually accumulates around it, and is leading to the spread of saltmarsh in

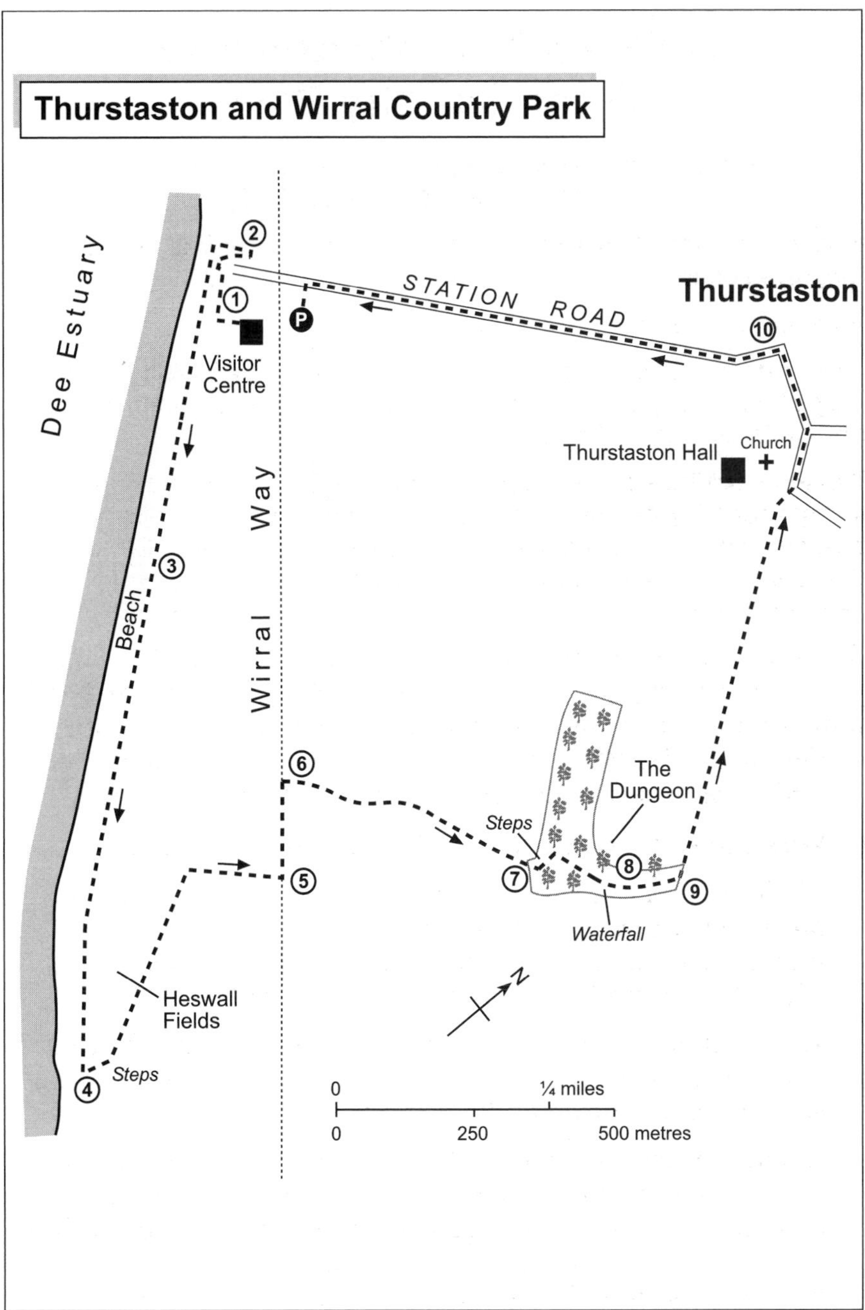
Thurstaston and Wirral Country Park
Dee Estuary
Visitor Centre
STATION ROAD
Thurstaston
Wirral Way
Beach
Thurstaston Hall
Church
The Dungeon
Steps
Waterfall
Heswall Fields
Steps
N
0
¼ miles
0
250
500 metres

The cliffs, made from clay and rocks

many places around Britain's more southerly coasts including the Dee estuary.

2. Go right, along the clifftop, to reach the road-end. Just beyond the bollards, take the path which soon descends to the beach.

Our route goes left, but before you do so, notice the area to your right at the bottom of the cliffs. This was probably the site of a port called Dawpool, mentioned in several documentary records 250 or so years ago, and previously known as Redbank. No maps exist to show its exact location but there's a neat row of sandstone blocks further along that perhaps marked a jetty.

Turn left at the bottom of the cliff to walk almost a mile.

The cliffs are made of a material called boulder clay or, technically, 'till'. Vast, thick icy glaciers once covered most of Britain, including the Wirral. Glaciers actually flow, like rivers, but very slowly. As they do so, they pick up and pulverise any rocky material they come across. The material that makes up these cliffs

Looking out to sea

– the boulder clay – was picked up from much further north in Britain and dumped here when the ice melted about 10,000 years ago.

As you walk along the beach you will notice pebbles of many different colours. These are broken and rounded fragments of rock mostly dragged here by the ice from the Lake District, Scotland and Ireland. How many different colours of pebble can you count?

For information on the birdlife see p.86.

3. Continue along the beach ignoring any steps to the left (at the time of writing there are no usable steps up the cliff, but one new set is planned).

The cliffs and nearby area have been designated by English Nature as a Site of Special Scientific Interest (SSSI). One of their attractions is that the cliffs are constantly wearing away, due to the action of the sea at their foot. This means that trees and shrubs have little chance to grow, but many less common smaller plants are able to colonise here. It is this wearing away that made the authorities decide that some of the paths down to the beach were too dangerous. You will notice great cracks in the cliff, and several areas where the land has slipped down to the base.

4. The cliffs gradually get lower and finally peter out where a small stream crosses the sand towards thickening clumps of cord-grass in the estuary. Go left here, up a sandy path, next to some boulders. After about 20 metres ignore a forking path to the left into a field – stay on the main path.

Heswall Fields to your left is a 40 acre/16 hectare National Trust site bought in 1978 as part of their 'Operation Coastline Campaign'. The Trust buys up stretches of coastline whenever it can to protect it against development. So far, it owns over 600 miles of British coast.

The last time I was here the hawthorn hedge to the left of the path had recently been laid – see page 55 for more on this.

5. When you reach the Wirral Way cross to the firm path and turn left.

The railway line that once ran along here opened in 1886. The last train used it in 1962, and in 1973 the disused line became the dominant feature of the Country Park – the first designated 'Country Park' in Britain.

6. After about 200 metres turn right, signposted to The Dungeon. Follow the path gently uphill.

The Dungeon – the name comes from an old local word meaning 'a wooded valley' – is an area of old woodland, dominated by oaks. It is steep and rocky and you can see a cave cut into the rock. It's not surprising that there are tales of smugglers using the area as place to shelter centuries ago.

7. Cross a small bridge on your left and climb the steps. Turn right at the top. Take care with young children here; there is a steep drop to your right for a little way.

If you are interested in rocks, stop a few metres after a dip in the path, just beyond a few holly trees, looking down the steep bank. Here is a superb example of a geological 'fault', which occurs when two sections of rock have shifted relative to each other. Down to your right, you can see the valley walls are made of red sandstone – solid, 'blocky', and rounded. But to your left the walls are made of stone sliced into lots of thin horizontal layers – 'siltstone'. The two rocks now but up against each other like mismatched wallpaper.

Soon you will come to a waterfall – small, and the only natural free-falling example on the Wirral (there is, though, a pretty water cascade in Walk 4). The waterfall occurs because water is only able to flow over *the underlying rock – siltstone. However, Wirral's predominant rock is sandstone, which is porous. This means that water normally filters* through *it.*

8. Continue along the path.

Old railway sleepers have been put to good use along this section.

9. When you reach a path-junction turn left. Continue, soon crossing a stile, and stay on the same heading to reach Thurstaston village.

Along the way, as the ground rises you get great views – to your right the spires of Liverpool's cathedrals; to your left, the distant mountains of Snowdonia. As you continue, you can see the Great Orme near Llandudno, and, on a clear day, Anglesey 50 miles away.

Thurstaston village is ancient and is mentioned in the Domesday Book, written in 1086. As you near St Bartholomew's Church you will notice that there is a tower in the graveyard. This is the only remains of a church built in 1820, and you can see the line where its gable end butted up against the tower. There was another ancient church before that one, and the current one was built in 1886.

The big building behind the church is Thurstaston Hall. The brick central section dates from the 1500s and other parts are even earlier. In the 1980s a gang of workmen found what was said to be a 'smuggler's tunnel' leading from the Hall towards the coast. The Hall is also supposed to be haunted, and the ghost once sat long enough for someone to sketch its portrait!

10. Follow the road as it bends to the left. 100 metres after the bend look right to admire the enormous barn.

It was built in 1862 and made of typical local materials – sandstone walls with a Welsh slate roof. It is, incidentally, also attractive at night, when it is lit up.

In about two-thirds of a mile you reach the car park on your left.

The old Thurstaston Station platforms are still visible on the coastward side of the car park. This was a single-track railway but with passing loops at some stations. The only significant accident on the whole line occurred at Thurstaston when two trains collided in 1957 and one railway employee was seriously injured.

Walk 14. Willaston

A restored railway station – a Roman road – old buildings – Wirral's largest windmill – an ancient hedge – the Wirral Way – farmland – a glow-worm site

Start and finish: Hadlow Road Station, Willaston.

Distance: 3¾ miles, allow 2 hours

Refreshments: Pollard Inn; The Nag's Head; Aston's tearooms, all in Willaston.

Walking Conditions: Generally good paths and occasional road. The track at point 8 can be very muddy after rain.

Allow time to look around Hadlow Road Station. It has been restored to how it looked in 1952, when trains ran on the line between Hooton and West Kirby. The display includes advertisements and tools; you can see the old ticket office and look inside the signal box.

1. At the road entrance to the station, turn right towards the village centre.

   After about 100m you pass Ash Tree Farm on your right, one of many very old buildings in the village. The earliest part of the farm, to the right, is made of sandstone and dates from the early 1600s. The cross-wing section, made of hand-made brick, was added in 1697. Further along is the E-shaped Old Hall, again probably built around the early 1600s.

2. Take a look at the 'Willaston' village sign a few metres on from the Hall, then cross the road onto the village green and aim half-left to the Memorial Hall.

   The village sign is said to be made of 'millstone grit', a tough form of sandstone forming much of the Pennines, and also found, nearer to home, across the Dee estuary in north Wales. It was widely used for grinding grain in mills – hence the name – and this stone came from the windmill we'll see later on the walk.

   Willaston is an ancient place known to have existed before the

Domesday Book of AD1086. In the Middle Ages, it gave its name to the administrative area – known as a 'hundred' – which covered all of the Wirral. It is possible that the representatives from all the Wirral's villages met on the green, which used to be much larger than it is today.

People have been living in the area much longer than this though: several axes used by prehistoric man have been found in local fields.

A plaque on the front of the Hall shows the position of several of Willaston's noted buildings. The beige building with light-brown timbers dates from 1631 and, for a while, was an inn called the Red Lion.

The copper beech, in the centre of the Green was planted in 1935 to commemorate the Silver Jubilee of King George V.

3. Go to the main road, and turn left to walk about 50m. Cross the road just before the churchyard and take the signposted path.

4. At the end of the churchyard wall, bear diagonally left, aiming for a break in another wall about 100m away, again signposted as a footpath. Follow this path through some trees, emerging by Jackson's Pond.

Take a moment to look at the field to your left – it has long dips and bumps in it which extend the other side of the tennis courts. These may be relics of old "ridge and furrow" farming (see page 61) or, perhaps, 19th century ploughing using newly invented 'steam ploughs'.

5. Go through the gate into Jackson's Pond (passing stands of reed mace or 'bulrushes'), and along the wooden walkway. At the far end, take the curving path right to emerge at Willaston Meadow and Woodland.

Go right or left to thread your way along the curving paths, to reach a wooden gate near the far end of the meadow.

This recently established award-winning site is managed as a community resource by villagers. Wild flowers have been sown to create a semi-natural grass meadow. Apple trees, and oak and

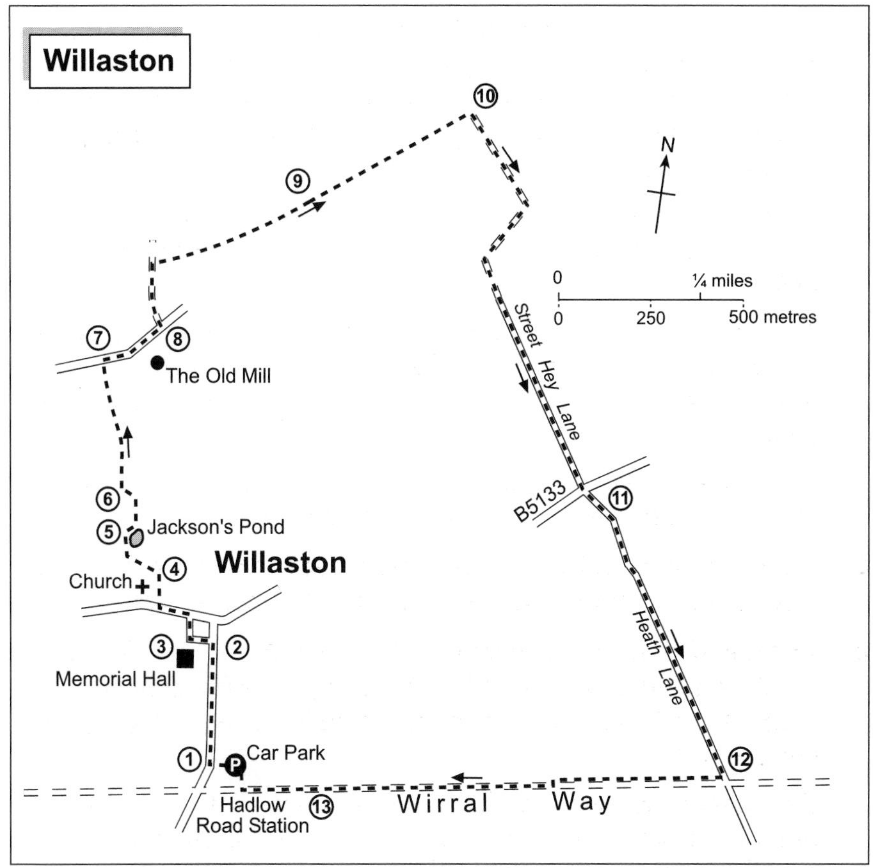

beech saplings have been planted, and stretches of new hedge made by local school children. It is hoped that a variety of wildlife will be attracted to the area.

There is an information board at the far gate with more about the development of the meadow and what it contains.

6. Turn right to reach a kissing gate. Continue, over a stile, and then over another at a road.

7. Turn right and walk about 150m.

There has been a mill on or near here since 1321. This mill – at 30 metres high, the largest on the Wirral – was built in 1800 and used to grind flour and, later, cattle food. It stopped being used in 1930 when the sails were severely damaged in a storm. You can see other buildings associated with the mill – the bakery, cart shed and stables – which have been turned into houses.

Willaston Mill: the largest on Wirral

8. Just after the mill, turn left along a track (there's a half-hidden signpost to "Raby"). After about 150 metres go up the stone steps to the right, over a stile and straight ahead down the side of the field.

   You can see Liverpool's cathedrals in the distance to your left, before the hedge starts.

9. Continue in the same direction, crossing two footbridges made of double railway sleepers.

   The large hedge to your left is ancient. Dating hedges is not a precise science but, as rule of thumb, for each woody plant species found in a 30-metre stretch of hedge, the hedge is 100 years old. Eight species have been noted in some stretches here, suggesting the hedge is 800 years old (and maybe more). Species I have noted along the stretch you are walking include oak, hawthorn, gorse, elder, holly, rowan, hazel, sycamore and willow. The next village up the Wirral is Raby, which is thought to have been the southern limit of where Norse settlers came to live around AD900. This means the substantial hedge may once have separated Norse and Anglo-Saxon Wirral. Today it marks the boundary between Merseyside and Cheshire.

10. At a stile and third bridge, made from a single sleeper, turn right onto a good path. Keep on the main path, which becomes a track and then a road.

You pass by several ponds along here – marl pits. These pits were dug for their sub-soil, which was spread over the nearby land as a fertiliser. The pits later filled in naturally with water. The fields off to the right were some of the earliest farming land in Willaston, in use in the Middle Ages, so the pits, which have gnarled and bent oaks growing around them, may be very old. There were complaints to the local court in the 13th century that 'dangerous' marl pits had been made at Willaston – these were probably dangerous to deer, which mattered more than people! See page 36.

This road is Street Hey Lane, believed to be an old Roman road from Chester's North Gate up the Wirral. The road was archaeologically excavated in 1960, with trenches sunk in several places just before the B5133. This revealed a layer of cobbles carefully laid on a sand and clay bed.

11. At the junction with the B5133, go straight over into Heath Lane. Continue along here for about half a mile.

12. Just before the road starts to rise, bear right. Then take the first path, signposted on your right. After 300m, the path joins the main Wirral Way – stay on this firm track.

If you had turned left, under the bridge, a few hundred metres further on there is a rare local site for glow-worms – rangers lead walks to track them down on summer nights.

The Wirral Way was opened in 1973, and was Britain's first designated Country Park. It follows the line of the old railway from Hooton to West Kirby, which closed to rail traffic in 1962.

13. A few hundred metres later take the right-hand fork between gate-posts to arrive back at the car park.

Walk 15. Hilbre Island

Great views – an old lifeboat station and signal station – rock caves and an arch – wildlife including seals – a weather station you can check at home – the site of dinosaur prints

Start and finish: the slipway near the north end of the West Kirby Marine Lake. Parking, buses and railway station nearby.

Distance: about 4 miles; allow 1 hour each way, plus stops (more with children).

Refreshments: none on the island.

Walking Conditions: flat, over sand, shingle and occasional rock, which may be slippery in one or two places; grassy paths. It should be possible to keep your feet dry! If there is a strong wind against you, it can make walking quite tiring.

Visiting Hilbre is a memorable day out, with lots to see, rock-pools, caves and beaches to explore, and masses of wildlife. Plan your visit around the tide times as Hilbre is cut off for several hours per day. Plan either to walk there and back during one low tide, or to stay there while the tide comes in and goes out again.

A notice board by the slipway gives full information on the tides as well as telling you much more about the island. Alternatively, call the Wirral Country Park Visitor Centre on 0151 648 4371 or 3884.

1. Do not walk directly from West Kirby to Hilbre as the sand is unsafe. Instead, walk towards the left-hand island, called Little Eye.

   Hilbre Island is the largest of four islands. Tanskey Rocks to your half-left are largely buried in the sand and invisible. Then there's Little Eye, Middle Eye (also known as Little Hilbre) and Hilbre Island itself. They are all areas of sandstone rock left sticking up 10,000 years ago after the melting of mighty glaciers that had carved out the Dee Estuary.

   The islands have been occupied since the Stone Age, and there was a Christian community based on them 1000 or more years ago. A

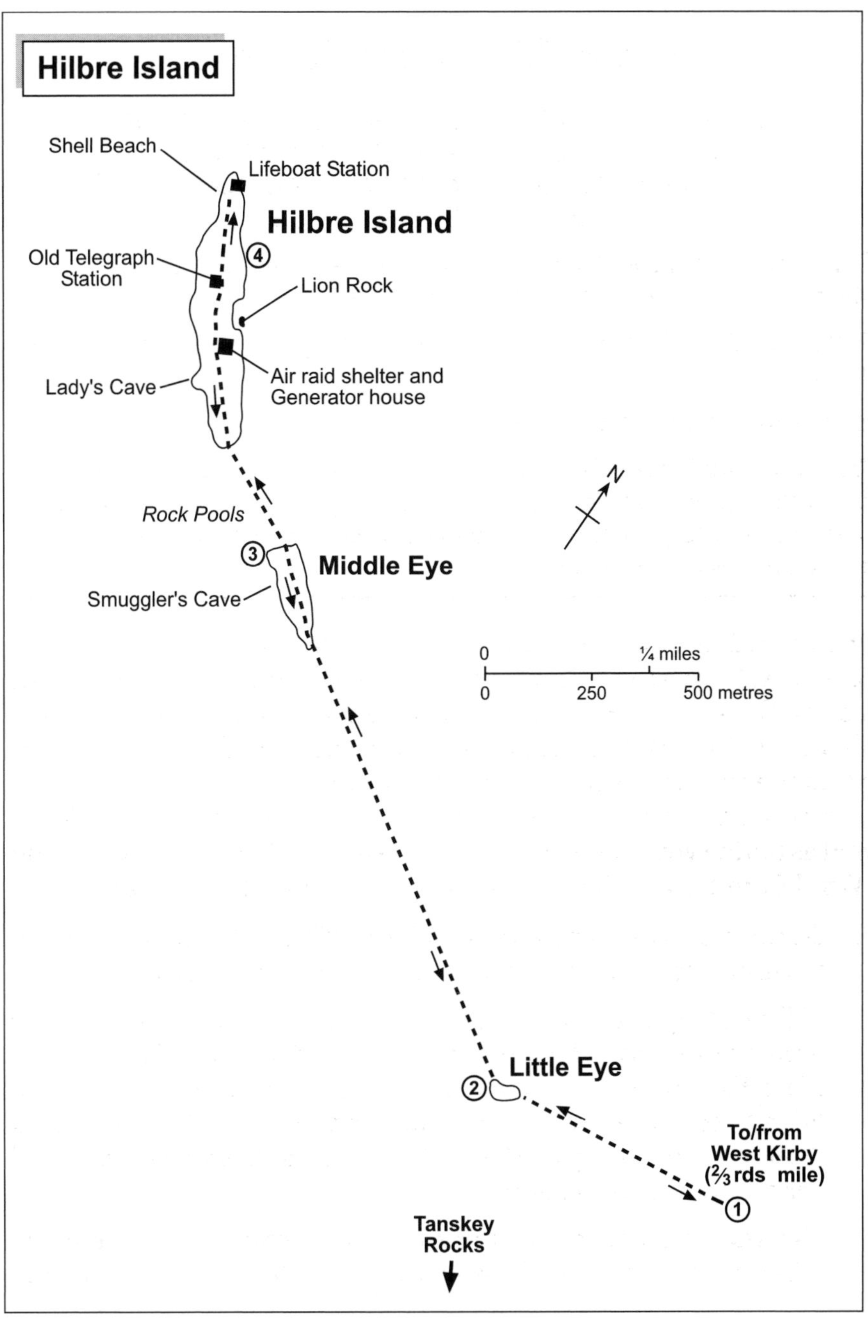
Hilbre Island
Shell Beach
Lifeboat Station
Hilbre Island
Old Telegraph Station
Lion Rock
Air raid shelter and Generator house
Lady's Cave
Rock Pools
Middle Eye
Smuggler's Cave
N
0
¼ miles
0
250
500 metres
Little Eye
To/from West Kirby (⅔rds mile)
Tanskey Rocks
1
2
3
4

cell of monks, enjoying the peace and isolation, used Hilbre until 1536.

As you cross the sand you will notice millions of little mounds of sand. These are the casts of lugworms who swallow the sand they live in, digesting the organic material, and ejecting the rest to make the cast. Lugworms, as well as other sand-living animals such as ragworms and various molluscs (shellfish), attract numerous birds to feed, which is why the Dee Estuary has been designated a Site of Special Scientific Interest. Birds that are easy to spot include curlews – with long downward-curving beaks; oystercatchers with red beaks, black upper body and white lower body; and redshanks – smaller and lighter-coloured than oystercatchers and with red beak and legs. Other important birds here include grey plovers, knots, dunlin and bar-tailed godwit.

2. When you reach Little Eye turn right and make your way to Middle Eye.

Middle Eye has lovely grassy paths which you reach from steps on the right-hand side next to a wave-cut tunnel in the rocks. On the left side of the island is Smuggler's Cave – the islands were said to be the haunt of smugglers and wreckers in the past. And on Hilbre itself you can find Lady's Cave where, legend says, a dying girl was cast up after throwing herself from a ship to avoid an arranged marriage.

3. Continue to Hilbre Island, past rock-pools where you may find crabs, to a path starting on the left-hand side of the cliff.

These rocks were formed over 200 million years ago when what is now Wirral was part of a vast desert. Footprints of a prehistoric reptile called cheirotherium have been found on Hilbre (and at Storeton Quarry – Walk 6).

As you walk up the path you will see wire cages, with open-ended funnels at one end. These are Heligoland traps used to catch birds for recording and ringing before being released.

Notice also a mound of grass on your right with a low brick chimney sticking up. This was an air raid shelter during World War II and also held an electrical generator. From here, a cable led to

The Old Telegraph Station on Hilbre

Middle Eye on which structures had been built with holes in the top. Lights shone through the holes to deceive German bomber aircraft that these were the factories of Liverpool.

The path takes you to the Old Telegraph Station. Built in 1841, it was part of a chain of signalling stations between Liverpool with Holyhead, sending messages about shipping. The next Wirral signal station in the chain was on Bidston Hill.

Immediately before the Old Telegraph Station is a tall mast. This is a radar station, a webcam and a weather station, part of the Liverpool Bay Coastal Observatory. Back home, log onto the Proudman Oceanographic Laboratory website (http://cobs/pol.ac/cobs/met/hilbre/) to get up-to-the-minute pictures and weather reports, including wind speed and temperature, from Hilbre.

To your left are steps. Near here is a shell midden – a mound of discarded shells from edible shellfish, left by prehistoric inhabitants of the island.

The old lifeboat station on Hilbre Island

Keep your eye on the water around the island: you are almost certain to see the heads of Atlantic grey seals bobbing around. They are also a common sight on the sandbanks in the distance to your left.

At the tip of the island are the remains of a lifeboat station, used until 1939. Originally twinned with Hoylake Lifeboat station, it was quicker at low tide for the Hoylake-based crew to travel to Hilbre and launch a boat there than to launch from the mainland. Note how there are two trackways – a switch mechanism enabled the crew to use the appropriate track for the tide conditions.

A tide gauge is operated via a pipe leading from the bottom left-hand side of the lifeboat station. It is vital that ships going in and out of the Mersey know exactly how much draught (the depth of water needed to float the ship) is available. The tide gauge gives this information precisely and up to the minute.

4. Return using the outward route.

Hilbre Island from the sands

If you have time, visit the 'Red Rocks' sand dunes behind West Kirby beach, another Site of Special Scientific Interest. They support a wide range of plants and animals – over 200 bird species alone have been reported. The very rare natterjack toad also lives here.

Walk 16. Leasowe

A lighthouse – a hovercraft tale – coastline – sand dunes – hay meadow

Start/finish: Leasowe lighthouse (off the A551, at the junction of Pasture Road and Leasowe Road, Moreton)

Refreshments: none en route.

Distance: up to 4 miles; allow at least 2 hours, but it is easy to cut short

Walking Conditions: level ground, suitable for pushchairs etc., except the optional eastern section using sandy/grassy paths over low hills.

This is a route for all the family with easy, flat walking. There is plenty to see but you can make it as short as you want by re-tracing your route at any time.

The walking route is within the boundary of North Wirral Coastal Park. Many of the Park's features are mentioned on this walk but you may also like to wander round Moreton Conservation Area (to your left as you face the sea from the lighthouse) which is a wildlife haven. It includes a pond, reed-beds and a wildflower meadow. The whole of the North Wirral Foreshore has been designated as a Site of Special Scientific Interest because of the variety of wild birds it attracts – especially noticeable at low tides as they look for food in the sand and mudflats.

The lighthouse has a '1763' date-stone above the doorway and the initials 'M.W.G.' after the then mayor of Liverpool, William Gregson. You can make out bricks under the whitewashed exterior – this is the earliest brick-built lighthouse in the country and is 30 metres high. It is regularly open to visitors who can climb the 130 cast-iron steps to the top. Originally there was another light on the seashore and, by aligning the two lights, ships could find the entrance to the channel that led to the Port of Liverpool. But the shore light collapsed, so a replacement was built on Bidston Hill in 1771, and ships' captains then aligned the Bidston and Leasowe lights.

1. After viewing the lighthouse, take the tarmac path up to Wallasey Embankment. Turn right.

Leasowe Bay (photo: Adam King)

The 3-mile-long embankment is just one of various types of sea defence that protect the north Wirral coast. Behind the embankment lie 18 square kilometres of land below the level of highest tides.

The shore here was one terminus of the world's first hovercraft passenger service – and possibly the shortest-lived! The idea was to run a regular service between Leasowe embankment and Rhyl in north Wales. The service started on July 14th 1962 but on the 14th September that year the craft lost an engine and then got badly damaged in a storm. The service never operated again.

After three-quarters of a mile you pass Leasowe Castle to your right (you cannot access it from the path). The original sandstone Castle was built in 1593, not as a defensive structure but possibly in connection with the nearby Wallasey horse races (there are several former race courses on the Wirral – see also Walks six, seven and twelve). The Castle soon became a ruin and was given a common name for such ruins – Mockbeggar Hall. The nearby shore is called Mockbeggar Wharf today.

The building was later restored and extended, and there are still hints of the past inside: the 'Star Chamber' is impressive with wood-panelled walls (the panelling actually came from the Palace of Westminster in 1836) and large hanging tapestries depicting the four seasons.

2. At the wide bay drop down to the shore, if the tide allows (or stay on the path if you prefer).

The bay is not an ancient feature. Unlike the rest of this coast this stretch has never been owned by the local authority so it did not benefit from the first coastal protection schemes. In the first half of the 20th century the dunes that covered this stretch receded by 85 metres, forming the bay. The breakwaters of piled-up boulders in the bay were constructed in the 1970s and 80s to limit the damage, and further boulders line the back of the shore. Most of the boulders are made of limestone that was formed on the seabed; you will quickly spot fossils of shellfish and coral in the rock.

3. At the end of the bay re-join the main path and continue to the far end of the parking area to a gap in the wall on the right by a National Cycle Network sign (for more on the sign see page 96).

Along the way have a look at the information board at the start of the parking area for information on birds you may spot when you return along the coast.

Retrace your steps from the cycle sign if you wish to keep to level ground, otherwise turn right and go down the access road until you reach a car park.

4. Go through the car park and, at the end, walk past the Notice Board to an information board which tells you about Gunsite Meadow.

This hay meadow is rich with wildflowers in summer, and is named after anti-aircraft guns sited here during World War II.

5. Take the diagonal path across the meadow to reach a wooden kissing gate. Take the main path, uphill. Later you will want to go left up the wooden steps about 75 metres after the gate, but first continue on the path to another information board.

After looking at the board you may wish to take a detour to wander around the dunes, which are an increasingly threatened habitat nationally. These ones are particularly vulnerable as the coastal defences stop them from being replenished with sand blown from

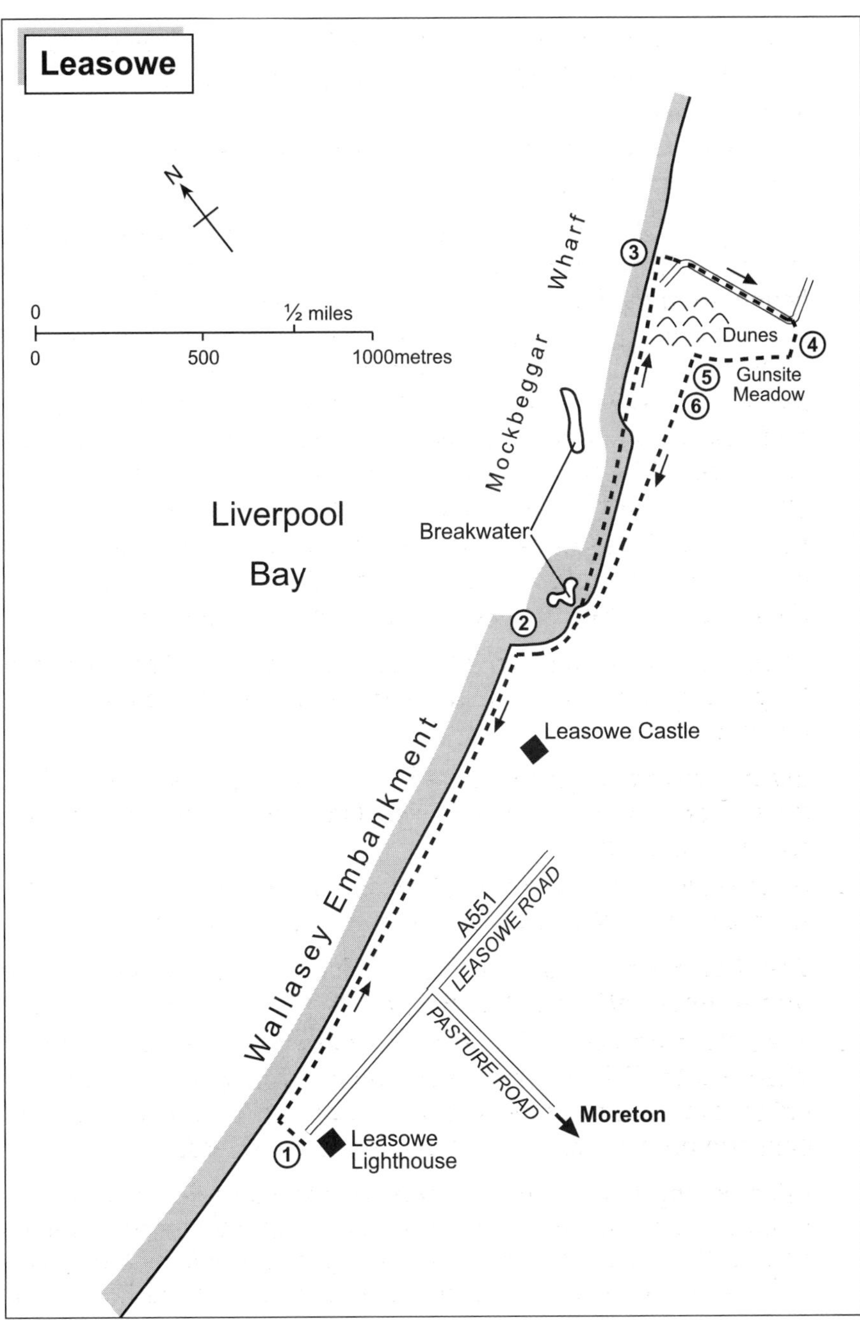
Leasowe
N
0
½ miles
0
500
1000metres
Liverpool
Bay
Mockbeggar Wharf
Breakwater
Dunes
Gunsite
Meadow
Leasowe Castle
Wallasey Embankment
A551
LEASOWE ROAD
PASTURE ROAD
Moreton
Leasowe
Lighthouse
1
2
3
4
5
6

The lighthouse

the shore. They are home to a number of animals and plants, many rare, which are mentioned on the board.

The commonest plant you will see on the dunes is marram grass and it is very important for the preservation of dunes. The plant has an incredible ability to grow really long roots, so no matter how high the dunes get, it can still tap down into the water beneath the sand (marram has been known to sit on 30 metre high dunes). It can also spread a long way horizontally creating a new bud whenever the sand overwhelms it. This network of roots and shoots helps bind the sand dunes together, limiting erosion. You can see areas of the dune that have been fenced off; new marram is being planted here to encourage the dunes to stabilise.

6. Return to the steps and, at the top, continue along this path. Keep to the main path along the centre of ridge.

This area is known as the 'Bund'. It used to be a rubbish tip but is now a lovely meadow. Skylarks nest here and you may see them soaring upwards and hovering, singing sweetly.

Eventually join the path above the shore and retrace your steps to the lighthouse.

If you want to know more about the oil and gas platform out to sea, *see page 104.*

Walk 17. Landican and Little Storeton

Ancient lanes – an air crash site – farmland – pretty hamlets – a puzzle for cyclists – old buildings – old farming methods

Start and finish: Torrington Drive, next to the roundabout where the B5138 (Pensby Road) meets the A551 (Barnston Road), ½ mile south of the main entrance to Arrowe Country Park.

Distance: 4 miles; allow 2 to 2½ hours

Refreshments: Basset Hound pub in Thingwall.

Walking Conditions: Some good tracks and road. Some of the fields can be muddy, especially the first half-mile of the route in winter – wellies or good boots are recommended. Alternatively, take Landican Road from the start point to join the route before point 3 in Landican.

This route passes through three quaint hamlets, and uses some ancient lanes. Most of the time you are surrounded by fields, so it has a very rural feel.

1. Take the footpath by the roundabout, signed to "Landican". Keep to the left-hand field boundary, between some stone gateposts. Later, cross a footbridge then a stile and continue straight ahead, across a field. At the far side go through a break in the trees, keeping in the same direction, keeping a line of trees to your left.

2. Pick your way through some bushes to reach a track. Follow this to a road and turn right.

   Landican is a very old Wirral settlement. It is mentioned in the Domesday Book of 1086 and at that time included a priest, nine villagers and four Frenchmen! (The latter probably came here as a result of the Norman Conquest 20 years beforehand). The lane you are walking down is sunken below the level of the land to the side, due to centuries of use. Also, see how the roots of mature trees have wrapped themselves around the stones of old walls on your right.

3. After 150 metres take the track signposted "Public Bridleway to Storeton" to the right. You stay on this good path – an old route known as Landican Lane – for 1½ miles.

This little lane would have given access to the fields for the people of Landican over centuries. Records of 1846 show that, as well as producing oats, wheat, potatoes and turnips, many of the fields were growing clover. Clover was a valuable crop for feeding sheep and cattle; it was also an important fertiliser in the days before mass-produced agricultural chemicals – bacteria in clover's roots can convert nitrogen in the air into a form that other crops can use for growth.

After just over half a mile (almost one kilometre) you reach a left-hand bend followed by a downhill stretch. The area around here was the site of Wirral's worst air crash, in 1944. An American Liberator aircraft was flying from Northern Ireland to Wiltshire when it exploded in mid-air. Wreckage was widely scattered but the bulk of it fell in the fields around this part of Landican Lane – there are still visible depressions in the fields where it struck. 24 US airmen lost their lives and a memorial to them has been erected in Prenton. The cause was never firmly established but an on-board explosion or a lightning strike were possible reasons; enemy action was ruled out.

Continue, going over Prenton Brook and crossing under the Bidston-Wrexham railway and the M53, to reach a road at Little Storeton.

This is a pretty corner of an ancient village. Look up the road that runs left. Grange Cottages, the row of houses on the left are made of Storeton sandstone, quarried in the woods three-quarters of a mile to the east. Storeton stone is much paler than the red sandstone you find elsewhere on the Wirral, and was a popular building stone. The village smithy once stood at the end of this row of houses.

Just after you reach the road note the cast iron Millennium Milepost, one of 1000 created across the UK for the National Cycle Network. The circular plate towards the top carries letters and numbers. These are part of a Millennium Time Trail: You can 'collect' the design by 'brass-rubbing' it. Piece together a selection of these rubbings to solve a puzzle (you do not need to visit all 1000 mileposts!). Contact Sustrans for more information.

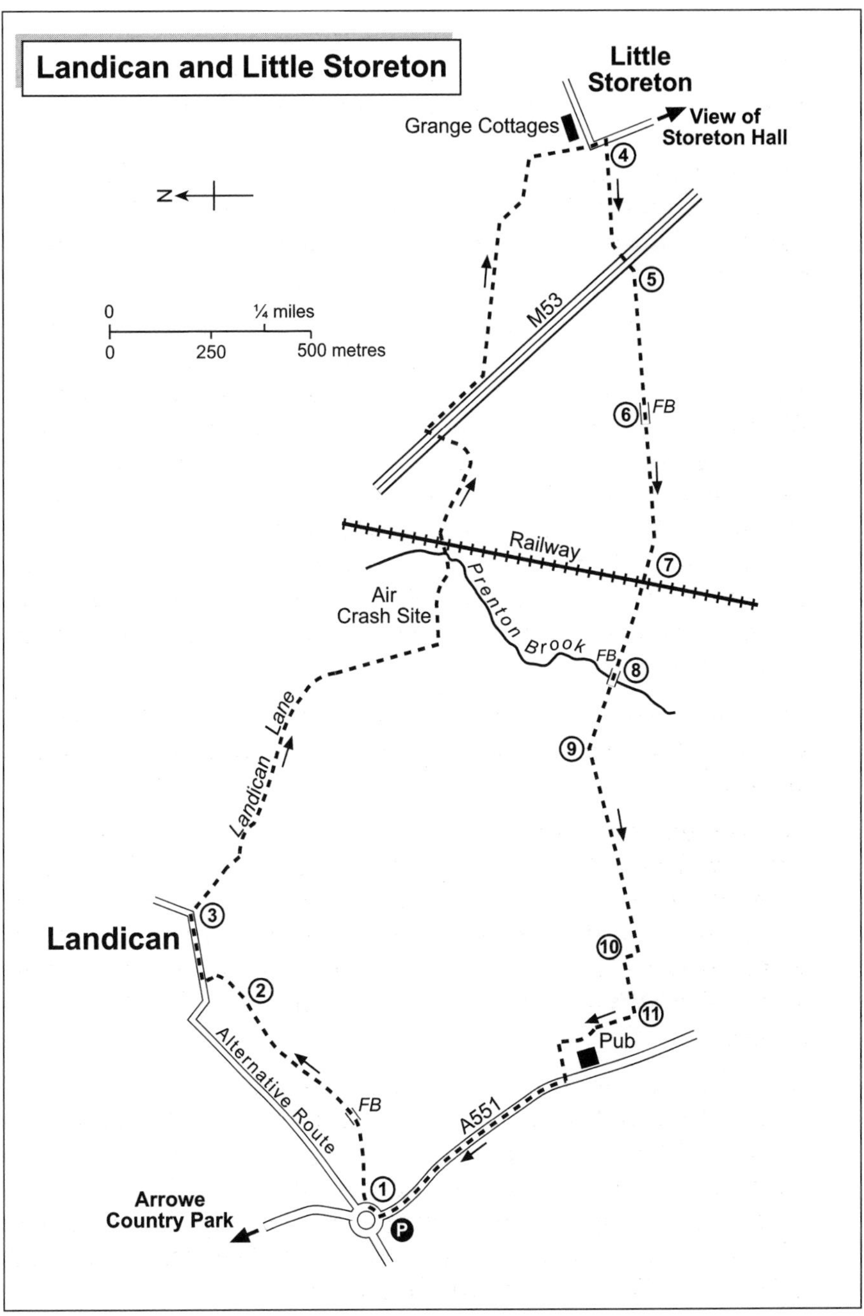
Landican and Little Storeton
Little Storeton
Grange Cottages
View of Storeton Hall
¼ miles
0
250
500 metres
M53
FB
Railway
Air Crash Site
Prenton Brook
Landican Lane
Landican
Alternative Route
A551
Pub
Arrowe Country Park
P

Barley field at Little Storeton

If you wish, wander 150m down the road to glimpse Storeton Hall over to your left (more information on page 35). Otherwise.....

4. 20 metres later, take the stile on the right and follow the path over the motorway bridge.

5. After the bridge, the path goes half-right to cross the field (it may look muddy but it is usually reasonably firm underfoot).

6. At the far side of the field cross a footbridge, then take the clear path that goes half-right, eventually going under two sets of electricity cables.

7. Reach the railway – cross with care! Continue straight ahead along a narrow path.

The track was opened in 1896 as part of the 'Dee and Birkenhead Railway'. There used to be a station 400 metres to your left – hence the road between Barnston and Storeton is 'Station Road'. The station closed to passengers in 1951. Next to the station there was once a brick-making yard, including large circular kilns to bake the bricks.

Notice the first stone gatepost you come to, about 20 metres after the track. It bears a symbol – a horizontal line with an arrow underneath. This is an Ordnance Survey 'cut benchmark' symbol – indicating a spot where the O.S. took a precise measurement of the height above sea level.

8. Go down a bank, over the stream and a stile and straight up the hill-side ahead, to walk to the left of some bushes that hide ponds. At the end of these, go diagonally right to reach a stile by a metal gate.

The ponds you pass are some of hundreds that stand out on maps, dotted all over the Wirral. Many of these were dug as marl pits in past centuries. Subsoil was dug and spread over surrounding fields; the nutrients from this subsoil were another way of increasing the soil's fertility, a method known to have been used by the Romans. Similar pits were also dug in places to obtain the clay for brick-making.

9. Walk alongside a hedge for two fields to reach a stile and path between hedges. Follow this path over another stile, to bend sharp right.

10. After 50m reach a track; turn left.

11. Reach a sunken lane. Turn right and stay on this to reach the main road.

You pass Manor Barn on your left – notice the water trough hollowed out of a block of sandstone, a water-pump and the three-step sandstone mounting block for getting onto horses.

Go right to return to the start.

Walk 18. New Brighton

Street art – a one-time entertainment mega-resort – coastal walking – a lighthouse – a pretty park – the Liverpool Bay oil and gas rig

Start and finish: Atherton St., New Brighton, at the Merseyrail station.

Distance: up to 4 miles; allow at least two hours but you can make it shorter by turning back at any time.

Refreshments: café at Vale Park; pubs and cafés in New Brighton and Harrison Drive.

Walking Conditions: tarmac paths and pavements throughout, suitable for pushchairs, cycles etc.

This is a route for a fine day, to catch the bracing sea air and great views. It's a one-way walk, made easy by hopping on a train at the far end to take you back to where you started.

Along the way you will find some excellent information boards about New Brighton in its heyday. There's also lots of street art to look out for.

The view you get from the station, downhill to the sea and across to Formby Point, would have been the first sight of New Brighton for millions of holidaymakers. The idea for the resort came from a Liverpool builder, James Atherton, who bought 70 hectares of sandy heathland to create a seaside resort fit for the cream of society. But over the decades New Brighton became a popular holiday and day-trip destination for people of all backgrounds.

Looking right, at the very top of the hill you can see a large Roman Catholic church built by a priest who wanted to match the great Basilica in Lisbon. It can hold 600 people.

1. Turn right from the station and left into Victoria Road. Continue in this direction to the seafront Promenade.

   The roadway after the traffic lights, with its wide pavements and rows of bright awnings, gives a flavour of New Brighton a century ago

2. Turn right along the Tower Promenade.

By the turning circle notice the carving on a block of sandstone, and about 30 metres later there's a ring of brass figures set into the ground, wearing granite clothing – dancing to '50s rock?

On your right is Tower Grounds where New Brighton Tower once stood. This tower, finished in 1900 and standing 189 metres high, was like Blackpool's – but much bigger. The grounds covered 14 hectares and offered fantastic entertainment for visitors – a 3,000 seat theatre, a huge ballroom, a water flume to ride down, a fairground, restaurants, gardens and much more. The tower only lasted 19 years but the entertainment complex hosted top acts (including the Beatles) until 1969 when it burnt down.

New Brighton Tower and Lake *(Reproduced by permission of Birkenhead Central Reference Library)*

Continue in the same direction, along Magazines Promenade

Stop to admire the nine metal disks, called 'Spray', by the entrance to Vale Park. Children will enjoy working out the pictures on them; and can you find the elephant?!

3. Walk about 75m up the road immediately after Vale Park, Magazine Lane.

On a corner is a house with the most extraordinary front gate you will ever see! This used to be the entrance to Liscard Battery, built as a defence for the Mersey, but never used in anger. Magazine Lane was named after an 18th century storage facility where ships unloaded their gunpowder before being allowed to enter the Port of Liverpool – they could not risk a huge explosion in the docks.

Go right and uphill a few metres to an entrance into the Park.

Spend some time exploring the immaculately groomed Vale Park which was opened in 1899 by the local council who wanted to create more open space for a growing population. Amongst other things, the park has a café, which houses a small display about the local area, a rose garden and a bandstand. This is still used for brass bands, pop concerts and children's shows. Unusual trees in the park include evergreen holm oaks (there's one immediately left of the café), a fig tree and a mulberry. A friendly local resident told me how, when she was a child, she used to climb the mulberry to collect its leaves, the staple food of silkworms that she kept at school.

4. Descend to the Prom and retrace your steps along it, maybe strolling along the sand if the tide is out.

Stop just before the large red buoy, marked 'pier'. New Brighton Pier jutted out into the Mersey here until it was dismantled in 1978. As well as offering its own attractions the pier was the unloading point for ferries bringing crowds of visitors from Liverpool.

A few metres later, on the other side of the road to the RNLI access ramp, notice a sculpture of guide dog.

This corner section of the Promenade was once a narrow strip nicknamed 'Ham and Egg Terrace'. This was the rough end of town, full of cheap eating palaces and dodgy characters. Drunken behaviour and crime made it unsafe for many to use. The Terrace was pulled down in 1913 and replaced with the promenade you see today, including the Floral Pavilion Theatre.

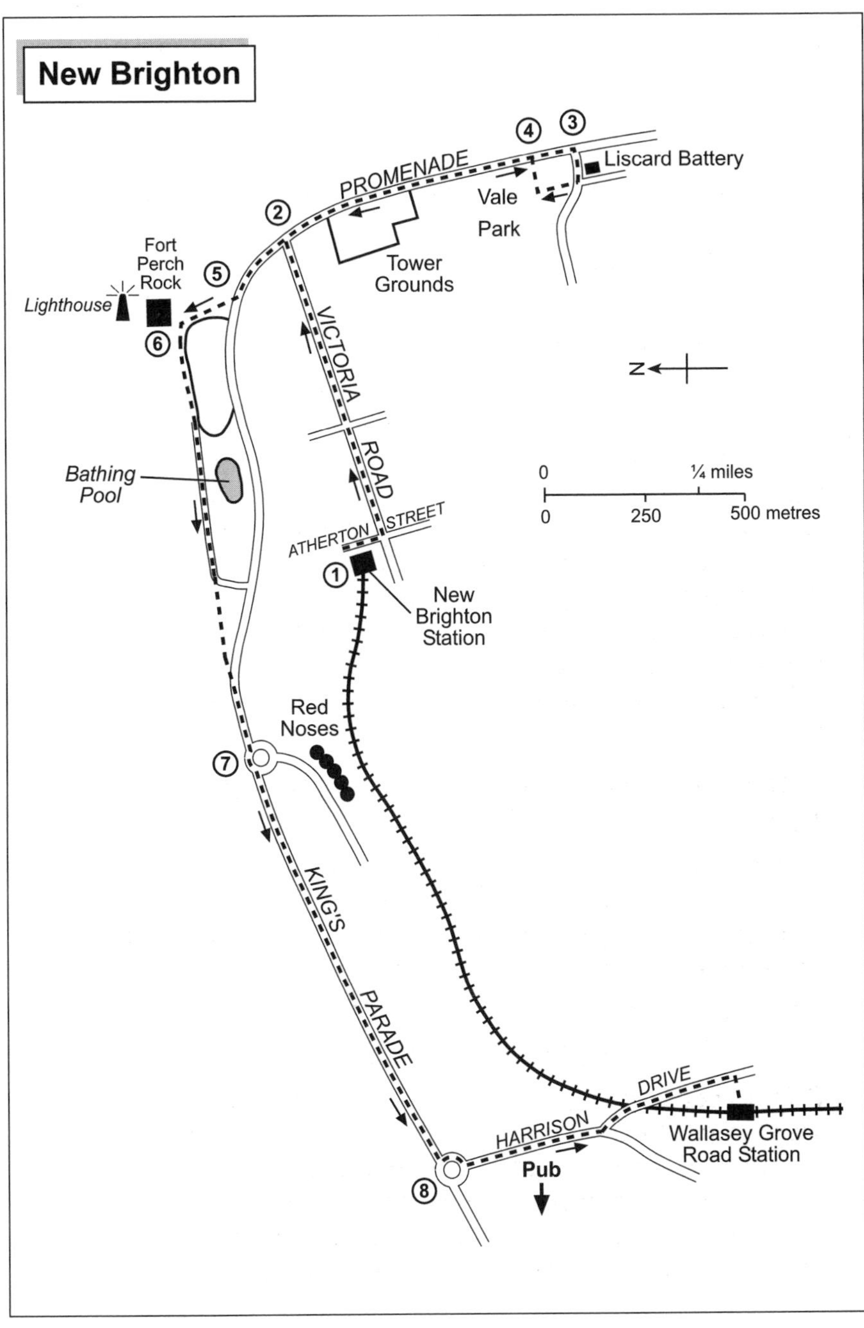
New Brighton
PROMENADE
Liscard Battery
Vale
Park
Tower
Grounds
Fort
Perch
Rock
Lighthouse
VICTORIA
ROAD
N
0
¼ miles
0
250
500 metres
Bathing
Pool
ATHERTON
STREET
New
Brighton
Station
Red
Noses
KING'S
PARADE
DRIVE
HARRISON
Wallasey Grove
Road Station
Pub

5. Fork right (note two more sandstone carvings), going to the left of Fort Perch Rock for a good view of New Brighton Lighthouse, and maybe exploring the rock pools between the two buildings if the tide allows.

Fort Perch Rock and the lighthouse were built on a sandstone outcrop that was a navigation hazard for shipping in and out of Liverpool. The rock was originally marked by a wooden structure or 'perch' but it was often washed away. It was replaced by the lighthouse, made of granite blocks, in 1830. Fort Perch Rock, meant as defence for Liverpool, was opened in the same year but never fired a shot in any battle. It did, however fire a warning shot across the bow of a ship that failed to identify itself in 1914 – the shot landed about 12km (7½ miles) away on Formby beach and was returned to the Fort!

6. Continue on the seaward side of the Marine Lake and on, to join the start of Kings Parade.

The huge basin to your left (after the marine lake) was once a world-famous bathing pool, almost 100m long, that could hold 3000 people, with another 10,000 spectators around it. It was irreparably destroyed by storms in 1990. Another great pool was built at the other end of the Promenade, just after point 8 on this walk, by the Derby Pool pub.

7. Continue along Kings Parade to the juggling clown sculpture, called 'Le Pierrot'.

It is extraordinary to realise that you are not standing on "solid ground" here. Red Noses to your left are the tops of cliffs that once dropped to a wide sandy beach below – another one of New Brighton's great attractions. But there were serious problems with erosion by the sea, so in the 1930s the high sea wall was built. The wide flat area before you, now covered by grass and Kings Parade, was made by piling material that was being dug out of the new Mersey Tunnel on top of the old beach.

To your half-right you can see the Liverpool Bay Douglas oil and gas complex in the far distance. Gas extracted from below the seabed is sent via a 34 km pipeline to a processing terminal at

New Brighton lighthouse

Point of Ayr, North Wales. Meanwhile, oil is piped 20 km from the drilling platform to a supertanker permanently moored away from shipping lanes. Here the oil is transferred into tankers for international export.

8. Turn left at the roundabout and take the left fork after 400m. At Wallasey Grove Road Station, catch one of the frequent trains back to the start.

Walk 19. Shotwick Village and Castle

A medieval castle site – an unspoilt village – a visit to Wales – the changing Dee estuary – woodland – farmland – ancient buildings

Start and finish: On the road near the church in Shotwick village. Shotwick is signposted off the A550, about one mile south of the 'Two Mills' crossroads.

Distance: 4 or 4½ miles; allow 2½ hours

Refreshments: none en route

Walking Conditions: mostly good tracks and fields and generally level walking; some woodland – short sections may be a overgrown in summer; two busy roads and a roundabout to cross – take great care. The fields after point 9 are often quite muddy.

This is one of my favourite walks and takes in what I think is one of the most evocative places in our area – the site of Shotwick Castle. The route is generally very peaceful and beautiful, full of historical and natural interest, with some superb views. Take care at the busy road crossings though.

Shotwick (pronounced 'Shottick' by the way) is a pretty and ancient hamlet worth taking time to explore. Once Shotwick was an important port, replacing Chester where the River Dee was silting up, and boats moored very close to the village. In the 1730s, the course of the Dee was changed to the Welsh side of the estuary and the land between drained by ditches.

There is information about Shotwick Village, including the church, Greyhound Farm and Shotwick Hall, in Walk 23.

1. Take the track through the 'Marsh Access Gate' to the left of the churchyard.

   Shotwick Bridge and the cobbled road by it were part of a medieval road called the 'Saltesway' used by Cheshire salt traders. Shotwick was an important place for traders as there was a ford here allowing the Dee to be crossed into Wales.

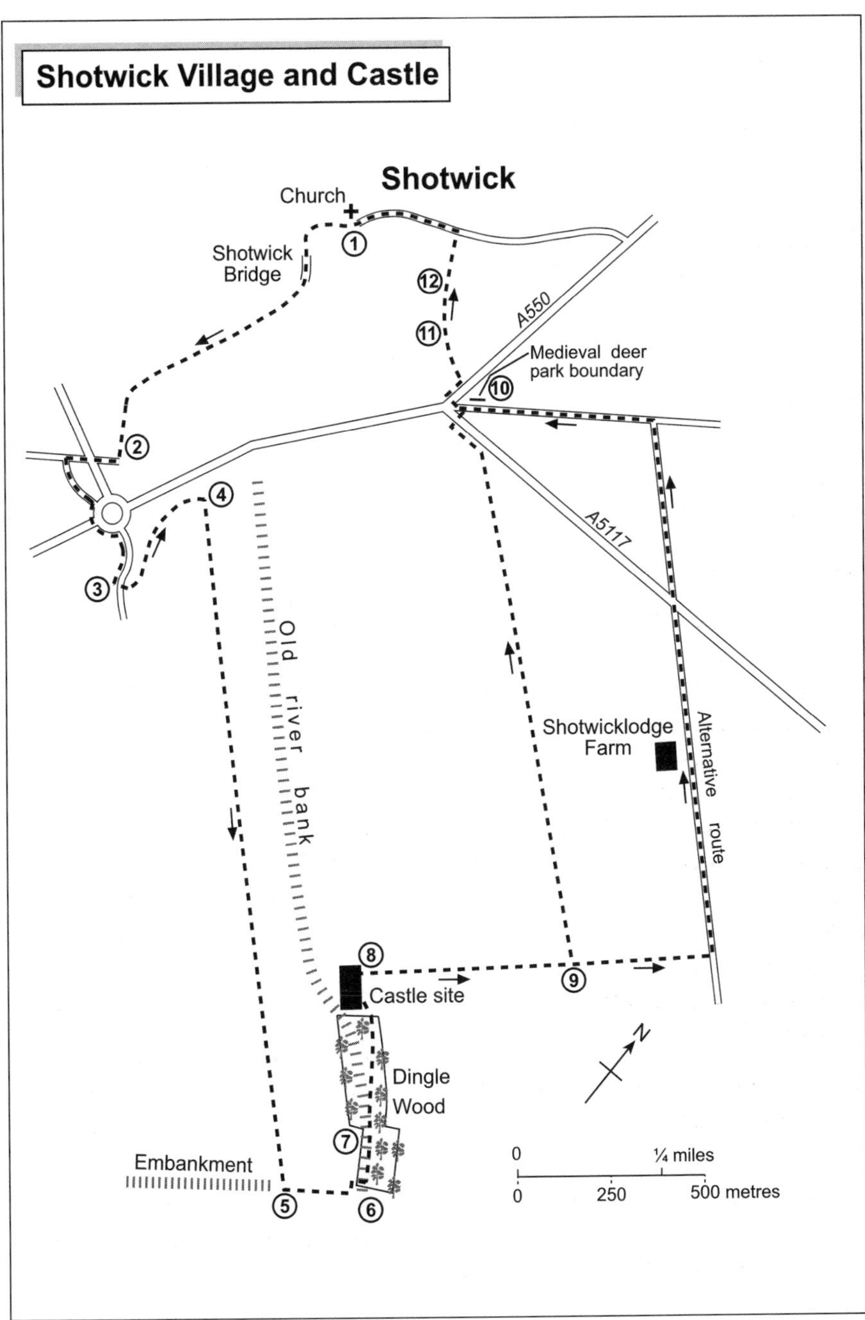
Shotwick Village and Castle
Shotwick
Church
Shotwick Bridge
A550
Medieval deer park boundary
A5117
Old river bank
Shotwicklodge Farm
Alternative route
Castle site
Dingle Wood
Embankment
N
0
¼ miles
0
250
500 metres

Continue along the track, around a bend. At the next right-hand bend, a gentle one where white poles stick up to left and right, you enter Wales.

2. Follow the track, past houses and through a tunnel. At the top of the rise, turn left. Go anti-clockwise round the roundabout and down Green Lane East. Shortly afterwards take the road signposted 'RAF Sealand'.

3. At the bottom of the short hill, go left, past concrete barriers and a gate, along a good track. (There is a short cut from just after the houses at point 2 to point 4, along a cycleway. However it requires a perilous crossing of the dual carriageway and is not recommended).

   RAF Sealand was originally a training base. Now it is the home for a maintenance unit working on electronic equipment for all three armed services.

4. Continue on the track until it bends sharp left. Turn off here and aim for a stile tucked in the corner a few metres away to your right. You may have to pick your way through low undergrowth to reach it. Cross the stile and continue straight ahead for just over a mile.

   Across the field to your left you can see the land rises: that used to be the bank of the River Dee until the course was changed. You are walking along the old course of the estuary and the fine soil covering the flat land around you is 'alluvium' – material washed down the river – which makes good agricultural land. To your right are the Clwydian hills stretching across the horizon.

5. Eventually you reach an embankment running off right with a scatter of Scots pine and larch each side. The embankment is part of an early 19th century scheme to prevent flooding and reclaim the land for agricultural use. Take the bridge to your left here (welcome back to England!). Walk initially with the drainage ditch to your right; when it bends right go straight ahead to a kissing gate and a track.

6. Turn left, then right just before a gate, through a gap in the fence. Immediately fork left, up the bank, then go left following a clear narrow path along the top.

The church at Shotwick

Trees and shrubs in these woods including ash, beech, elm, sycamore, hawthorn, oak, and blackthorn. Non-native rhododendrons can look attractive but, in time, can overwhelm everything around them destroying the woodland.

7. Continue on this path, crossing a wooden bridge, after which it leaves the edge of the bank. After more woodland, and an overgrown path through bracken, you reach the site of Shotwick Castle.

Nothing remains of the structure of the castle today, but the massive earthworks, including an inner and outer moat, suggest a very substantial building. A motte and bailey castle was built here first by the conquering Normans, 900 years or so ago. The stone castle was built later to defend the English-Welsh border and was used by English kings to support their attacks on Wales in the 12th and 13th centuries. The castle may have been pentagonal in shape and was built right against the estuary so that ships could moor alongside it. Today, osiers (willows) sit in the damp ground below the castle site. In 1327, a deer park was created at Shotwick and,

Part of the moat that once surrounded Shotwick Castle

with the threat from Wales gone, the castle was turned into a hunting lodge. It never ceases to amaze me how, very frequently, every trace of large old buildings has disappeared – with the materials used elsewhere. Recycling is certainly not new!

Keep your eye open for buzzards – I have seen them wheeling above me here a couple of times.

8. With your back to Wales cross the stile at a fence corner to your half-left. Walk straight on to the second gate, near which you will see a footpath signposted left, over a stile.

9. For the main route (which is shorter and gives an easier crossing of the A5117 at traffic lights), cross the stile and follow field edges to take you to the main road, point 10. (There is an old 'Beware of the Bull' sign along this route. I have only once seen a bull here; it was with cows and paid our large party no attention whatsoever. Bulls are not usually aggressive when cows are around, and farmers are generally conscious of the need not to put dangerous animals in fields where walkers go. Nevertheless, you should treat any bull with respect.)

For the alternative route (to pass Shotwicklodge Farm) carry on up the fields to a quiet lane, and turn left.

Shotwicklodge Farm was home to the keeper who managed the medieval Shotwick deer park. It once had a moat, and the interesting buildings include a massive barn. It is thought to date from the late 1500s which means that the timber uprights you see were sawn around the time of Elizabeth I – and come from a tree growing much earlier than that.

If you are following the alternative route: Cross the dual carriageway with extreme care. Straight on along the lane, and left at the end.

If you are interested in the medieval landscape wander a few metres up Woodbank Lane to the footpath sign pointing left. In front of you is a ditch and bank – made as part of the northern boundary of Shotwick deer park.

10. Cross two main roads at the lights; walk right for 60 metres and take the kissing gate to your left. The path is unclear but aim for a gate a few metres right of the far telegraph pole.

11. After a second gate follow the right-hand field boundary, dropping down a bank which leads to a footbridge.

12. Go uphill to a gate; straight ahead to a second gate to go left at the lane back to Shotwick.

Walk 20. Backford & the Wirral Canal

An historic road – a canal, boats and bridges – old buildings – farmland

Start and finish: By the telephone box in Backford (off the A41), about 3 miles north of Chester.

Refreshments: None en route; the Bunbury Arms, Stoak, is a nice pub if you extend the canal walk by 1km/0.6 mile each way

Distance: 4¼ miles; allow 2½ hours

Walking Conditions: Mostly flat, on good surfaces. 1 mile across field-paths.

This is a gentle, rural walk with a 'transport' theme. The late 18th century was a period of great change in the Britain as the industrial revolution took hold and the country's transport network was transformed. This walk follows two features of that developing transport system – a road and a canal.

Centuries earlier, Backford had marked the southern limit of the administrative region, known as the 'hundred', that covered the Wirral.

1. From the car park, go left, past the church.

   Part of the church dates back to the 1200s. Its tower was added in about 1500 and is one of four within a 10-mile radius of Chester built to an identical plan; the others are at Shotwick, Handley and Tattenhall. Note the gargoyles and also the eight pinnacles on top of Backford's tower – if you do either of the walks through Shotwick (walks 19 and 23) you'll see the pinnacles are missing on Shotwick's tower, probably knocked down during religious upheavals in the 16th century.

   Go left again at the A41. Continue for 750m/half a mile.

   The A41 (as well as the A540 running along west Wirral) was a 'turnpike', opened in 1787, leading up the peninsula from Chester. Turnpikes were roads operated by business trusts that built and maintained them in exchange for tolls charged to users. Previously

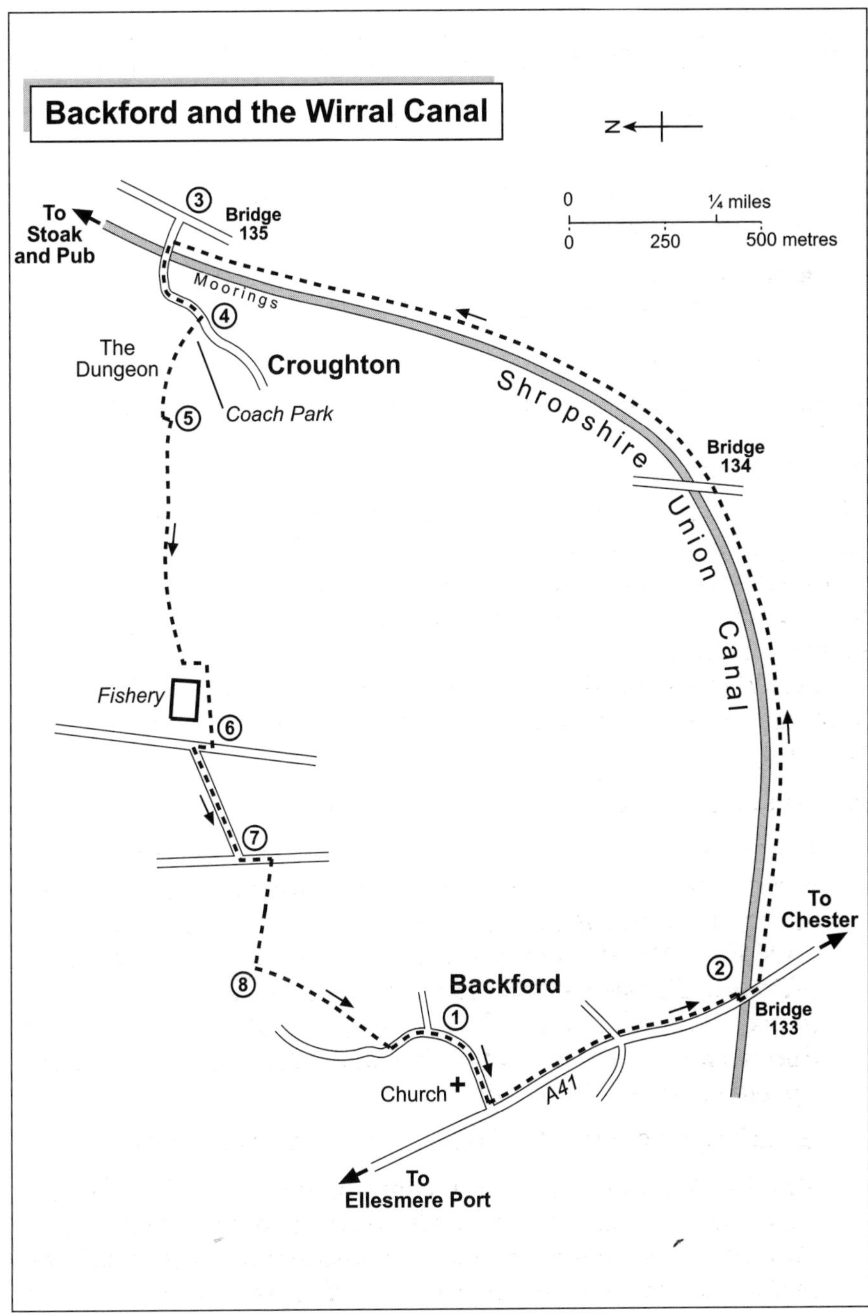
Backford and the Wirral Canal
N
0
¼ miles
0
250
500 metres
To Stoak and Pub
③
Bridge 135
Moorings
④
The Dungeon
Croughton
⑤
Coach Park
Shropshire Union Canal
Bridge 134
Fishery
⑥
⑦
⑧
Backford
①
Church
A41
②
Bridge 133
To Chester
To Ellesmere Port

the cost of maintaining roads had to be met by the local community but transferring the costs to road-users, via the trusts, meant rapid growth in the quantity and quality of roads. The improved network was a great force for economic expansion across Britain.

Horse-drawn passenger coaches frequently used this important road between Chester and the ferries across the Mersey at Eastham and Birkenhead. The nearest tollgate was situated half a mile/750m beyond where we leave the road, at Moston, where the road forks by a petrol station.

(Readers with a sense of irony may like to ponder the extent of change over the past 200 years: at Moston, where tolls were once collected from road users directly to improve the transport infrastructure, modern-days tolls are now collected in the form of excise duty at petrol pumps – but how much of it goes to improve the lot of today's travellers?!)

2. Cross over the canal, then go down the steps to the left, and continue ahead.

Bridge 134 on the 'Wirral Canal'

This section of the Shropshire Union Canal was known as the Wirral Canal when opened in 1795 by the Ellesmere Canal Company. They wanted a freight link from the textile-producing communities in Shropshire (around Ellesmere) and mid-Wales, to the Dee and Mersey. At the time, there was no village where the canal met the Mersey; the settlement that grew up there became known as 'Ellesmere Port'. The great civil engineer Thomas Telford planned the canal using a winding route that followed the contours, avoiding any climbs or falls. This made locks unnecessary, speeding the journey of the canal 'flyboats', and making the route very popular for passenger traffic to and from Chester.

The valley that Telford's route followed is known as the 'Backford Gap' or 'Deva Spillway' and was probably carved by meltwater from glaciers plunging south at the end of the last ice age, about 10,000 years ago.

Each bridge is numbered. You have joined at Bridge 133 – Bridge 1 is in Wolverhampton, 67 miles away (the canal became linked to the industrial heartlands of the Midlands in the 19th century).

Look for grooves on the brickwork on the inside edges of the canal bridges. These were carved by ropes used by horses to tow the canal boats. Also, notice the opposite side of the bridges reinforced by large blocks of stone to protect against knocks from narrowboats.

Rope marks on a bridge from when horses pulled the narrowboats

Go under Bridge 134.

Chester Zoo is at the top of the hill to your right. In still weather, boat owners moored on the canal can sometimes hear strange animal noises drifting through the air.

Continue, past boat moorings.

3. At Bridge 135 climb to the

The bridge at Croughton, designed by Thomas Telford

lane, cross the bridge and continue walking into Croughton. (For the pub at Stoak, continue on the towpath to Bridge 136. Cross over the canal and continue for 400m).

Croughton is an ancient village mentioned in the Domesday Book of 1086. There are several old houses and barns here.

4. After 250 metres look for a footpath to the right, over a footbridge, by a coach yard (another 'transport' link on this walk!). Walk up the yard (try to keep to the right-hand side, but it may be blocked). At the top corner of the yard, cross the stile and continue ahead, passing a steep-sided sandy valley called 'The Dungeon' to your right.

'Dungeon' is an old local word meaning a wooded valley. There is another steep-sided valley called 'The Dungeon' in Walk 13 at Thurstaston.

5. Soon, cross another stile and go left from a footbridge. Do not go through the metal gate but walk up the long field keeping the hedge on your left. Eventually cross another stile and 200 metres later turn left for 40 metres, then go right (passing a private fishery to your right), and continue ahead to a road.

6. At the road junction, continue straight ahead, along a road.

7. Bend left with the road. After 75 metres cross a stile set into the hedge on the right. Cross slightly right to the corner of the hedge ahead, then continue with the hedge on your left.

When I last walked this route these fields were sour-smelling and an unnatural grey colour. They had recently been spread with pulped newspaper, which I have noticed on many other local fields. The pulp enriches the soil and is meant to be ploughed in soon after spreading.

8. After about 300 metres, look for a stile and footbridge tucked into the hedge on your left. Cross, and walk ahead aiming for a stile by a large tree to the left of farm buildings. After the stile, continue straight ahead past various temporary fences to a stile by a tree at a road. Go left, back to the car.

Walk 21. The 'Lost Village' of Hadlow

A 'lost' village – Roman, medieval and turnpike roads – a restored railway station – farmland – unusual trees

Start and finish: pull-in opposite New Hey Lane, on Hadlow Road, ½ mile south of Willaston (or at Hadlow Road Station).

Distance: 4½ or 5¾ miles; allow 2½ or 3 hours

Refreshments: pubs and café in nearby Willaston; vending machines for drinks, sweets etc. at Foxes Farm.

Walking Conditions: flat; mostly good paths and tracks. Occasional muddy sections.

This walk, mostly through quiet farming country, takes us across an area of mystery. It also gives a taste of several types of road and track spanning 2000 years of history, and visits a railway station restored to its 1950s look.

1. Cross Hadlow Road and walk up New Hey Lane. After 200 metres take a path right. Follow this to another stile, and continue in the same direction.

   A place called Edelaue is mentioned in the Domesday Book of 1086. The fields where you are walking have the peculiar name of "Adler" – pronounced similarly to Edelaue. This, and other evidence, has led local historians to suggest that there may once have been a settlement here, which was deserted hundreds of years ago – no one knows why. The remains have now vanished but the local name "Hadlow" comes from the other names.

2. Continue straight ahead, through the trees and alongside a wall. Cross a stile and on to another.

3. Continue ahead, down a field, to cross a stile and gateway. Go left to reach another stile. Turn right and follow the field boundary, past a pond, to reach the A540.

   Have you noticed how there are often trees, generally oaks, spaced along the hedgerows? This is typical not just of the Willaston area,

Hadlow Road Station

but elsewhere on the Wirral too. Throughout most of the 19th century, there was a huge demand for oak bark, which was used in Wirral's many leather tanneries. The trees were planted to meet this need and were meant to be felled. But demand suddenly dropped when mineral salts became used for tanning instead, and the trees were just left to grow.

4. Turn left for 500 metres to reach a metal gate to the left.

The line of the A540 has existed since medieval times, maybe longer. In 1787, it became a turnpike. These roads were operated by business trusts that built and maintained them in exchange for tolls charged to users. Previously the cost of maintaining roads had to be met by the local community but transferring the costs to road-users, via the trusts, meant rapid growth in the quantity and quality of roads. The improved network was a great force for economic expansion across Britain. A tollhouse was situated on the corner of Badgers Rake Lane, 500 metres beyond point 5.

The brick block on the pavement a few metres beyond the gate is a

The ponds and tree-lined hedges around Hadlow are typical of much of the Wirral landscape

mounting block, used for getting on and off horses for riders leading their animals over the road.

5. Go through the gate and then over a stile. Keep to the field edge to reach another stile.

   As you go through the field from the road, on your right are a line of Austrian pines and Italian poplars, both often used as windbreaks. The bark of the poplars appears to have been severely nibbled by grazing animals.

6. Continue in the same direction to a big field. Walk straight across; the path may be indistinct but aim for a wooden post sticking up on the far side (in the past I've found that the farmer has grown his crops across the path; you are within your rights to walk through these crops provided you stick to the line of the path).

7. At the far side of the field turn right and soon go left up a track to Foxes Farm.

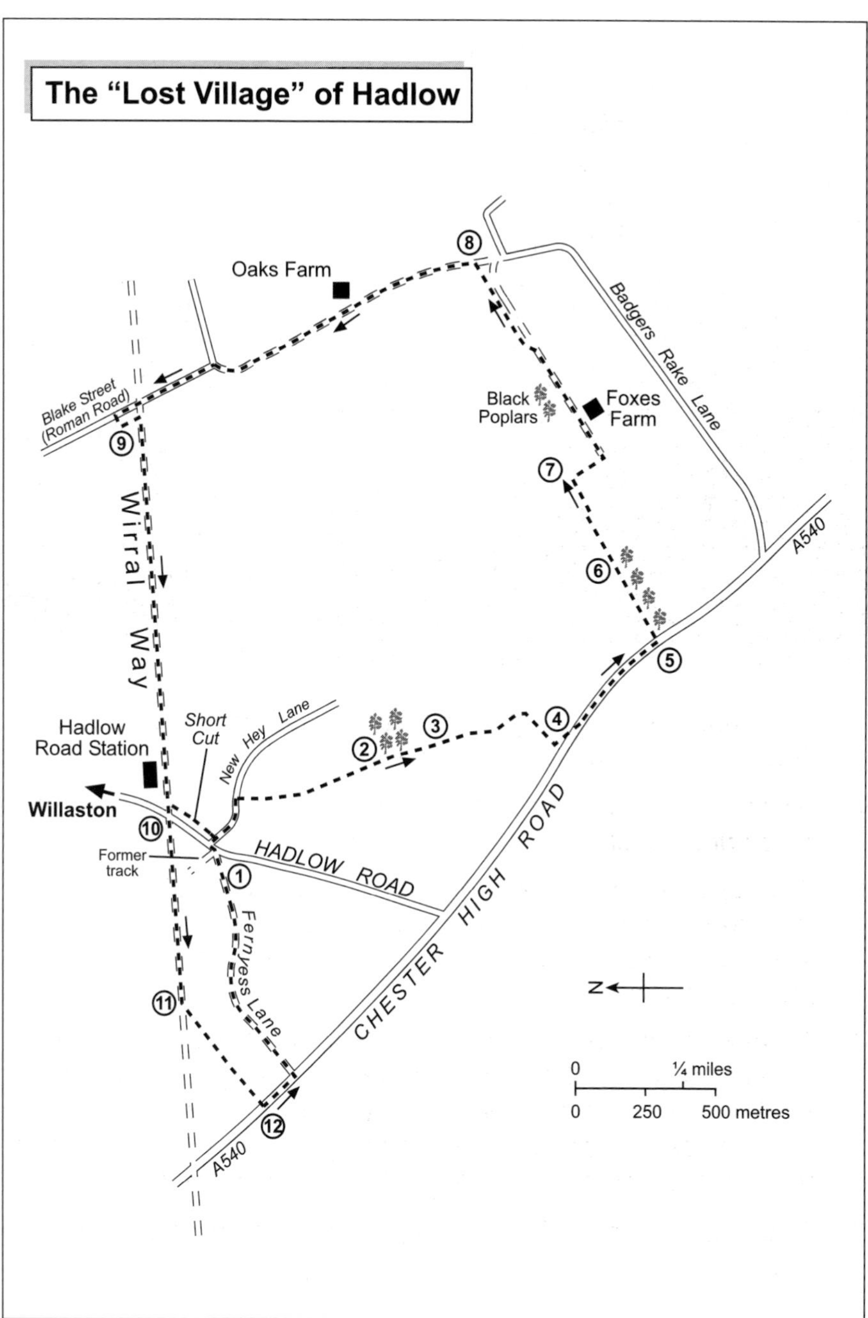
The "Lost Village" of Hadlow
Oaks Farm
Badgers Rake Lane
Black Poplars
Foxes Farm
Blake Street (Roman Road)
Wirral Way
A540
Hadlow Road Station
Short Cut
New Hey Lane
Willaston
Former track
HADLOW ROAD
CHESTER HIGH ROAD
Fernyess Lane
N
0 ¼ miles
0 250 500 metres
A540

The farm has popular riding stables. Vending machines with light refreshments are available here.

At the farm, continue ahead along a metalled track.

Almost immediately you pass three bungalows to your right. Look left here, across the field to a copse of trees. This is a designated Site of Special Scientific Interest as it contains black poplar trees, probably Britain's most endangered native tree. This site is a particularly special as there is a pair of male and female trees here, one of very few such sites in the country. The seeds are regularly collected to help grow new trees elsewhere. Black poplars like wet conditions and these ones live in a marl pit (see page 99 for more about marl pits).

Continue along the metalled track. After a while switch to a signed track that runs parallel to the track, along field edges.

8. At the T-junction with a farm road, turn left along it. After about 1km (0.6 miles), continue in the same direction when it reaches a minor road, to go over a hump-backed bridge.

The line of the road ahead is believed to be part of a Roman Road called Blake Street that went from the North Gate of Roman Chester up the Wirral. It can be traced through most of the Willaston area and at some points before and afterwards. There were archaeological excavations along it in the 1960s.

9. After the hump, double back and turn right along the Wirral Way.

The Way, Britain's first Country Park, was opened in 1973 following the path of the disused railway that had been built in 1866. The station was given the name "Hadlow Road" to avoid confusion with another station at Willaston near Nantwich. The platform area, signal box, booking office and waiting room have all been restored to how they looked in 1952, four years before the last passenger train drew up here (the line remained open for freight traffic until 1962). There is also a short section of track, though the station actually had two platforms and two tracks, which merged into one at each end of the station.

10. For the short cut, go left up Hadlow Road back to New Hey Lane. Alternatively, continue along the Wirral Way.

11. Take the kissing gate on your left, down steps, just after the pylon to your right. Follow the field boundary right until shortly before the telegraph pole; fork left along a ridge of slightly higher ground towards a cream-coloured house at the end of the field. Cross a stile, and another to reach the A540.

12. Go left for 200m and then left again through a metal gate, up a clear track. Continue back to the start.

This extra loop is included for you to enjoy the "green lane" of Fernyess Lane. This is an old track, certainly 250 years old, and was almost certainly a medieval route to Ness (the name means it was the 'fern-covered lane to Ness'). From the Chester High Road, it led to the crossroads, where this walk starts. Here, Hadlow Road, New Hey Lane, Fernyess Lane and another track, now vanished (see map), once met. Perhaps it was a major junction to access the mysterious Edelaue?

Walk 22. Little Neston & Ness

Wirral's only coal mine – disused railway lines – a deep railway cutting – ancient lanes – woodland – saltmarsh – the Wirral Way

Start and finish: Car park at end of Station Road, off mini-roundabout in Neston.

Refreshments: The Wheatsheaf, Ness and The Harp, after point 7. Good picnic spot near point 9.

Distance: 4½ miles; allow 2½ hours

Walking Conditions: Mostly easy walking over paths and tracks. Short sections near 3, 4, 8 and 9 can be very wet and muddy, so make sure you have appropriate footwear.

This is probably my favourite local route. The diversity of landscapes is extraordinary, from ancient tracks to remnants of the industrial revolution; and from a woodland haven to the grand expanse of the Dee saltmarsh. Each time you walk it, you will find something different to see.

1. From the car park walk under the railway bridge and up a residential road.
2. At the top of the road cross straight over, through a wooden gate and down the slope.

   You are entering the amazing 800m railway cutting built in 1866 as part of the Hooton – West Kirby line, now part of the Wirral Way. On either side rises sandstone, the intersecting sloping layers of which were laid down by water flowing through a desert over 200 million years ago. Everywhere you can see shallow cuts in the rock, made by the picks of the 19th century navvies who carved out the cutting. The gradient is 1 in 72, considered steep for the steam trains at the time of building. They often struggled to climb the hill or to control their descent.

   At the first of two bridges, both stained by locomotive soot, look for roman numerals carved into the stones each side of the arch. These helped the builders position them in the correct sequence.

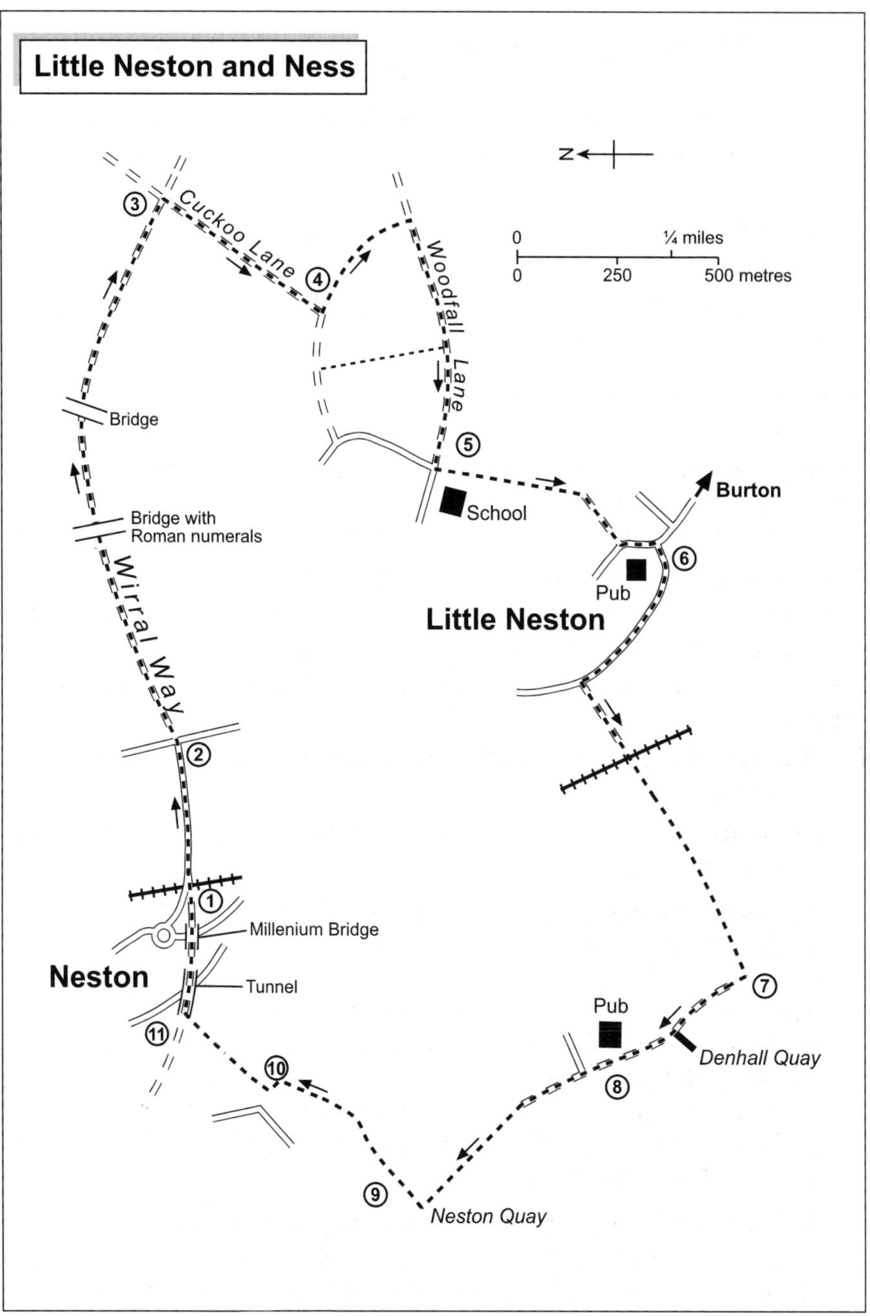
Little Neston and Ness
N
0 ¼ miles
0 250 500 metres
Cuckoo Lane
Woodfall Lane
Bridge
Bridge with
Roman numerals
Wirral Way
School
Burton
Pub
Little Neston
Millenium Bridge
Neston
Tunnel
Pub
Denhall Quay
Neston Quay

The cutting is dark and wet, suitable for only a few types of plant including ferns, ivy, mosses and liverworts.

For more on the Wirral Way, see page 68.

Soon after the path levels out, you pass ponds to your left. These are marl pits, dug by local farmers since medieval times for their fertile sub-soil which was spread over nearby fields. Water has filled most old marl pits, turning them into ponds. You will find similar ponds all over the Wirral.

You then reach a section of railway embankment passing through beech and sycamore woodland. This is a lovely area at any time of year and always seems to be full of birdsong.

3. Shortly before a narrow wooden bridge, go right down some concrete steps, over a stile, and turn right onto a track, Cuckoo Lane (this section can be very muddy – you may find slightly drier ground at the edges of the track). A little later, at a metal gate, continue up the hedged track.

Cuckoo Lane oozes antiquity. It is part of a local network of ancient tracks used for cattle droving and packhorse transport. Centuries of use have turned the route into a 'holloway' – a sunken track – up to 2 metres deep in places. Notice how it dries out as you climb from clay underfoot to sandstone.

4. At the top of the hill, turn left through a metal kissing gate. Follow the field boundary to a stile and continue down the narrow path. At the track (Woodfall Lane), turn right.

Most path boundaries around here are built with high banks reinforced by sandstone blocks. These ensured that livestock driven up and down the old lanes did not stray into the adjacent fields, damaging crops.

5. At the tarmac road look for a path to the left, before the school. Follow it to a stile and cross the field using the clear path bending slightly right. At the far corner, cross a sandstone block into Cumbers Lane and continue ahead to the main road.

Cumbers Lane is named after 'encumbrances' or obstructions once

Denhall Quay

found in the fields here. These obstructions were probably boulders.

Turn left to pass (or visit!) the pub.

6. Immediately after the pub, go right, down Well Lane. Continue for 300m to a track on the left with a small footpath sign, opposite 'New Heys'. Continue downhill for 800m, ignoring the paths into the housing estate.

   As you descend look ahead to the first line of hills in Wales. On the rounded brown hilltop sits Moel y Gaer, an Iron Age hillfort featured in Walk 24.

7. Eventually reach a path T-junction. Turn right and soon join a track.

   After about 150m you come to Denhall Quay, jutting left. The sandstone quay was built in the 1760s to serve Ness Colliery (also known as Denhall Colliery and several other names). The mine operated on the land around you from about 1760, driven by the developing needs of the industrial revolution, to 1927 when it had become uneconomic. The narrow coal seams were worked for almost two miles under the Dee and, in the early days, barges transported the coal along underground canals. They were propelled by 'legging' – people lay on their backs and pushed against the low roof. The coal was never of very good quality and was mainly used to power steam engines – almost certainly including the trains that chugged up and down the line along the Wirral Way, creating the soot you saw earlier.

Other industries sprung up nearby – brick-making, metal ore smelting, and quicklime production for building and agriculture. The limestone was brought to the quay from North Wales and the remains of the kilns for heating it are just visible as grassy mounds in a garden behind the pub. Children as young as seven worked the mine and the labourers lived in appalling housing, described in 1847 as 'the most miserable ... mass of hovels' on the Wirral. The pub's walls are lined with pictures from the mining days.

8. Continue in the same direction, past a metal gate, keeping parallel to the marsh.

The ground around here consists largely of spoil from industrial activity. But to your left lies the great openness of the salt marsh. If you could cross to the river you'd notice a succession of plant types each adapted to the increasingly salty conditions found as the estuary's waters get closer. Here though, you soon pass huge stands of freshwater-loving common reed (the type used in thatching roofs) rustling in the wind. Today the marsh has a wild beauty, but the estuary has been unforgiving. Many people drowned before the marsh was formed as they misjudged the shifting sands while trying to cross to Chester or North Wales.

Eventually you reach a well-worn stone stile. This is the site of Neston Key (also called the New Key and the Old Quay!), the site of another anchorage overtaken in importance by the port at Parkgate, and eventually stranded. (The sandstone wall about 100m further on, after a stream, is a lovely picnic spot). As you turn away from the marsh here, immediately on the right, you can see the remains of a brick building – The Key House – that served the port.

9. Turn right, away from the marsh, soon going between parallel hedges. Eventually cross a wooden footbridge. Cross the next field – the direct path across the field is often waterlogged so it is probably best to take the right-hand edge alongside the stream. At the top of the field go left a few metres, then right through a kissing gate.

10. Take the path ahead past a telegraph pole.

The line of hedges to left and right by the telegraph pole marks the disused railway branch line to Denhall Colliery.

Go straight ahead, up the field, to reach a kissing gate.

11. To return to the car park turn right along Wirral Way.

You may first like to look at an unusual little tunnel which the Way passes over. For this, cross straight over the Way from the field path and then go right a few metres down the road. Afterwards retrace your steps to the Way and continue over the Millennium Bridge, with its railway decoration and poetry, to the car park.

Walk 23. Puddington & Shotwick

A menagerie – ancient villages – a large pigeon house – the medieval landscape – redwood trees – masons' marks

Start/finish & Refreshments: The Yacht at Two Mills on the A540

Distance: 5¼ miles; allow 2½ to 3 hours

Walking Conditions: Roads, tracks and field-paths (can be very muddy after rain between points 3 and 5).

These are two of Wirral's most ancient and attractive villages, both recorded in the Domesday Book of 1086. Puddington has two large Halls. The older one was owned by the Massey family, who were surrounded by tales of intrigue and derring-do for 500 years. Shotwick, with its ancient church, was once a main crossing point into Wales and also a major port. The site of its castle is featured in Walk 19.

This Walk has a little more road-walking than usual, but the lanes are quiet and the surrounding country attractive.

1. Cross the A540 and turn left. Pass the grounds of a boarding kennels with its permanent private menagerie including alpacas, ostriches, rheas, pygmy and angora goats, and a Vietnamese pot-bellied pig called Claudia!

The A540 is an old turnpike road. See page 112 for more details.

2. 250 metres before the traffic lights, by the large road sign, cross the dual carriageway and go down Walden Drive. Go through a gate, and straight ahead over two stiles. In the works yard, keep to the left to reach another stile at the A550.

3. Cross with care, go left 15 metres, then through a kissing gate (I hope you're thin!) and over a stile. Go straight ahead, keeping the fence on your left, to cross a stream.

This is Shotwick Brook, which rises in Neston and once flowed into the Dee just below old Shotwick Bridge (which we cross on Walk 19). West-flowing streams are rare on the Wirral. Almost all the other streams and rivers eventually flow into the Mersey.

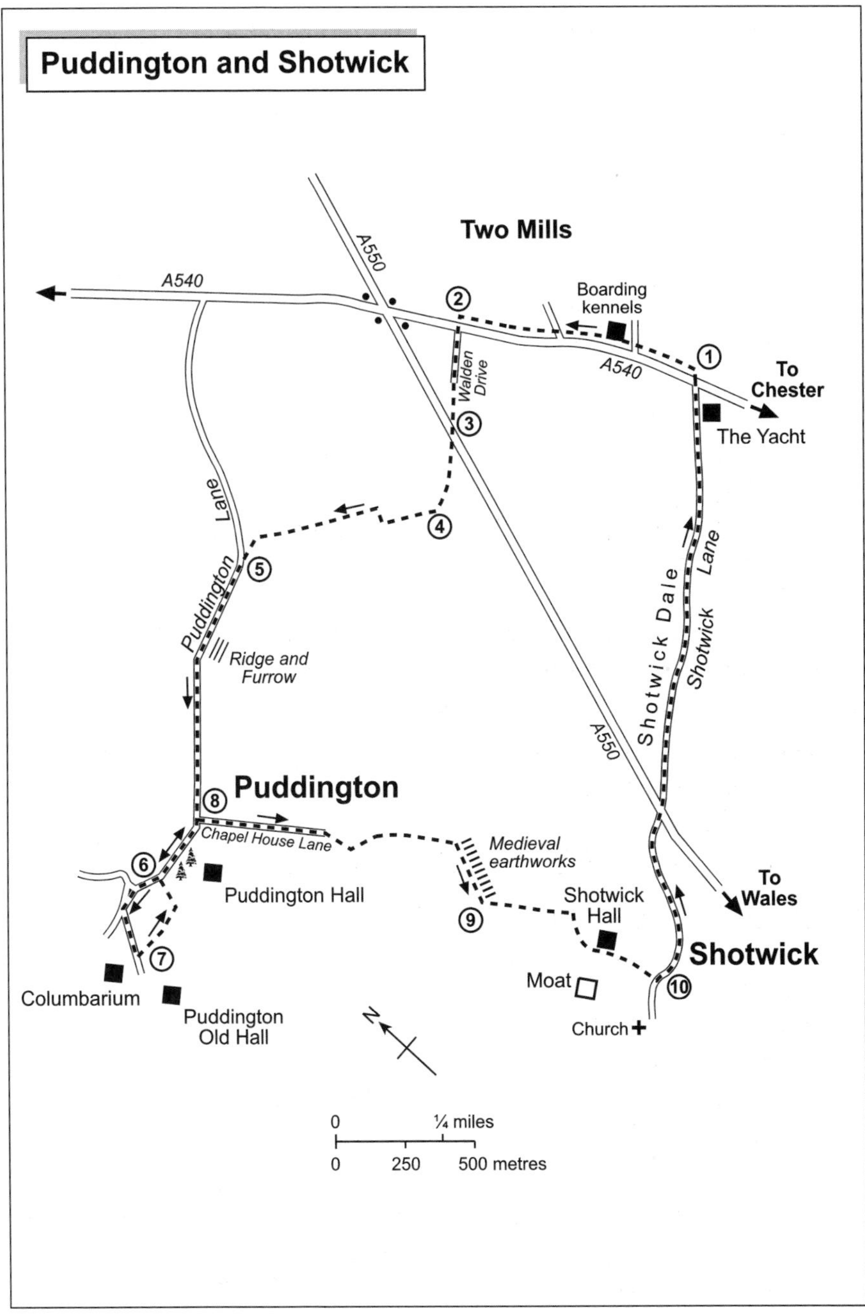
Puddington and Shotwick
Two Mills
A550
A540
Boarding kennels
Walden Drive
A540
To Chester
The Yacht
Lane
Puddington Lane
Shotwick Dale
Shotwick Lane
Ridge and Furrow
A550
Puddington
Chapel House Lane
Medieval earthworks
Puddington Hall
Shotwick Hall
To Wales
Shotwick
Moat
Columbarium
Puddington Old Hall
Church
N
0 ¼ miles
0 250 500 metres

4. Turn right, and walk for the next 650 metres/700 yards keeping the field boundary (variously a ditch, hedge or fence) to your immediate right all the time. You bend left after the house and eventually cross a stile to reach the road.

The columbarium (pigeon house) in Puddington

5. Turn left and continue to Puddington.

   Note the unusual thatched house opposite the stile, with thatched ducks on the roof!

   After 'Allsprings' look at the field on your left – there is a wide gap in the hedge about 150m after the house. It has strips of a 'ridge and furrow' farming system, parallel to the road, of a type used across Wirral in medieval times (see page 61 for more details). Continue, and later glimpse Puddington Hall through the trees, with parts dating from 1760. There are two magnificent Californian redwood trees at the entrance to a driveway, next to the Hall's converted stable block (the name of the tree comes from its bark which is, purely incidentally, fire resistant!).

6. In the centre of Puddington, keep left of the telephone box, and follow the road round left.

   After 100m, stop by the telegraph pole on your left. The long building ahead of you, slightly left, is Puddington Old Hall, the oldest part dating from 1490, (although it does not look particularly old from this angle). It was built around a courtyard and once had a moat. In the Middle Ages, moats were not necessarily a means of defence, but were common status symbols

Converted farm buildings in Puddington

amongst the better off. The Hall was owned by the Massey family for 700 years. One famous tale relates to William Massey who left the Battle of Preston in 1715. He rode the 46 miles home hell for leather, crossing the Mersey where it could be forded in those days, between Speke and Hooton. When he arrived at Puddington his exhausted horse is said to have dropped dead on the flagstones.

To your right is a squarish brick 'columbarium', or pigeon house – one of only two on the Wirral. Pigeons were popular winter food until about 1800, when almost all farms had a pigeon house. Pigeon houses fell out of favour when the development of winter root crops meant that animals could be kept and fed over the winter – previously most were killed in the autumn and their meat was dried and salted. As well as being a food source, pigeons also supplied dung – guano – which was a valuable fertiliser (and an ingredient for gunpowder!). This columbarium is odd in having corners that are not quite square.

7. Take the path left. This leads you back to Puddington Lane – turn right, retracing your earlier steps for 250 metres.

8. Go along Chapel House Lane. Stay on the road, eventually forking right (following a footpath sign). 100 metres later go left alongside a hedge. At the hedge-end, go half-right to pass right of a pond. Continue to the field edge and turn right.

To your left are a ditch and a bank topped by a substantial hedge. These are probably medieval, marking the ancient boundaries between Burton and Shotwick parishes.

9. After 200 metres turn left through a double gate. Keep the fence to your right, through a gate and eventually join a track. Follow this as it bends right, and go on into the village.

On your left you pass the picturesque E-shaped Shotwick Hall, built in 1662. This replaced an earlier Hall situated amongst the trees 125 metres to your right. The building has disappeared but the moat that surrounded it remains.

Take time to explore picturesque Shotwick. Most of the houses have great character, and the church has many fascinating features.

Look for Greyhound Farm: if you are looking down the road towards the church it is just after the Victorian post-box in the wall on your left. This was once the Greyhound Inn and became notorious as the place where runaway lovers were married illegally by the local curate – a kind of English Gretna Green.

Shotwick church is fascinating and there is not space here to cover everything. There is some excellent information dotted around inside the church – here are a few other unusual things to notice.

There has been a stone church here since Norman times. The wall each side of the porch, made of uneven sandstone blocks, is almost 1000 years old, as is the carved stone archway above the main door. The inside of the porch itself has several vertical grooves. These are said to date from the 1300s when Edward III banned football and made everyone practice archery on a Sunday after mass instead. The grooves are said to be where the archers sharpened their arrows.

A mason's mark in Shotwick church

Stonemasons used to leave individual distinguishing marks on the stones they cut. If you enter the tower, you can see one immediately on your right, at about eye level. Several others are visible elsewhere on the tower walls (see illustration). This tower was built in about 1500, around the same time and to the same plan as the towers at Backford (Walk 20), Handley and Tattenhall (all in West Cheshire). Several of the same mason's marks can be seen at all four churches, showing that the workmen travelled to where the work was.

10. After exploring the village go up the road. Cross Shotwick Brook (again), and then, carefully, the A550. Continue uphill, through pretty Shotwick Dale, back to the start.

Walk 24. Halkyn Mountain Common

Mining landscape – an Iron Age hillfort – great views – a different perspective on Wirral – quarrying – lime kilns

Start and finish: gravelled area on bend just above the church in the centre of Rhosesmor village. For Rhosesmor take the signed turn off the northbound A55 just after the Little Chef on your left. Go left at the Britannia Inn and then left at a T-junction onto the B5123. Continue for about 1¾ miles.

Distance: 6½ miles (for a shorter version, explore all or part of the high ground between points '1' and '8'); allow 3 to 4 hours

Refreshments: pubs at Rhosesmor and Rhes-y-cae but they are usually closed at lunchtimes. Point '8' is a good picnic spot.

Walking Conditions: mostly grassy paths and firm tracks. Occasional road.

'Compare and contrast' they used to tell us at school, and this route certainly gives you a completely different perspective on Wirral, starting across the Dee in the first line of hills in Wales. Not only are there magnificent views across to Wirral, and beyond (take binoculars if you have them), but you also get a fascinating and diverse landscape in its own right, with many points of contrast to our own.

The route is criss-crossed by other paths or tracks, so don't worry if you lose the suggested route occasionally – just take a logical route between the main landmarks.

1. From the parking spot, walk up the steep track which, by Rock Cottage, becomes a grassy path alongside a quarry.

There are fossils in the fence-pillars of the quarry, which is small compared to the vast, still-worked ones you will spot later. (Incidentally, if you hear a siren sound, they are about to blast some rock in one of the quarries). The underlying rock throughout this walk is limestone – older and harder than the sandstone that Wirral is made from. The same limestone also forms the Great Orme at Llandudno, and Eglwyseg Mountain above Llangollen. Limestone is used as building stone, and also yields lime, used in

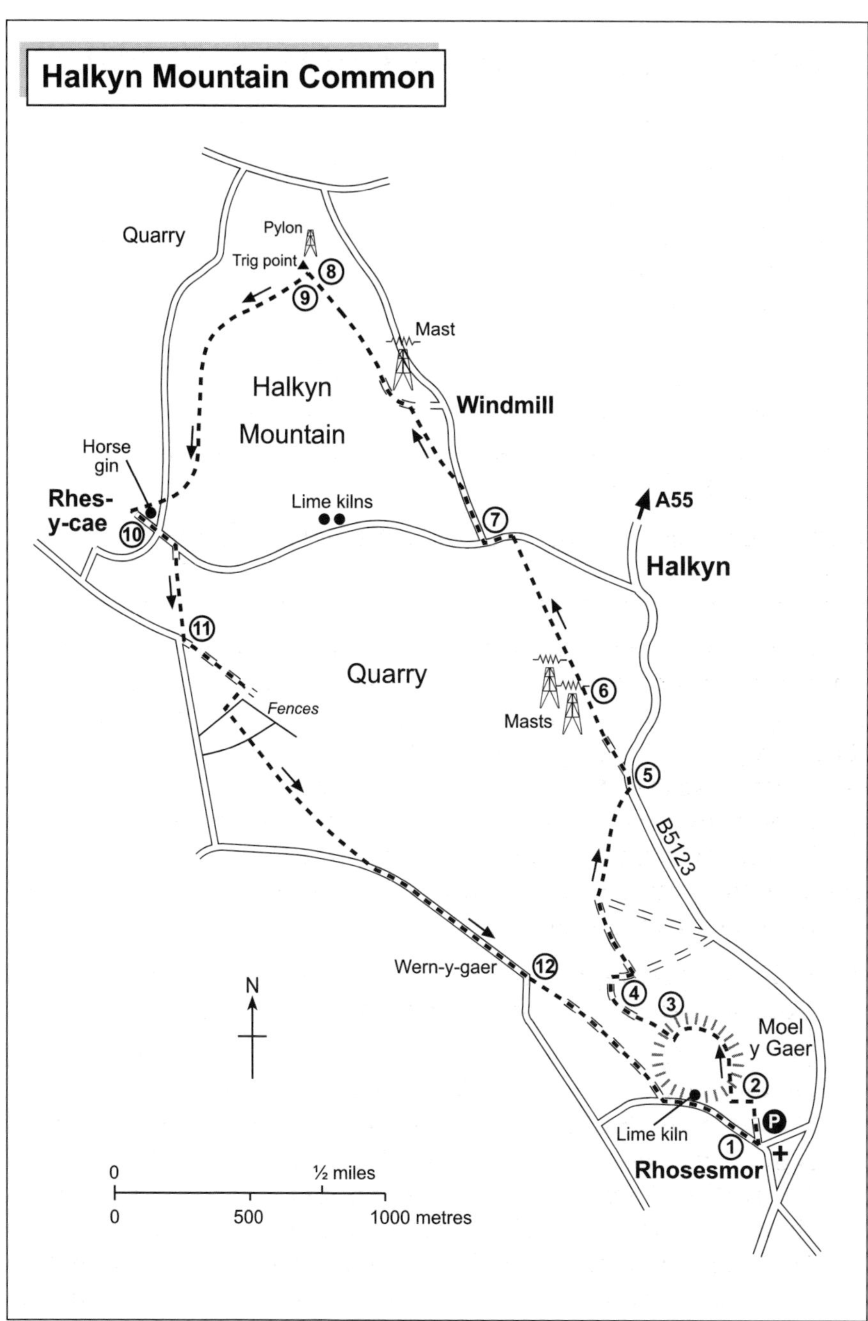
Halkyn Mountain Common
Quarry
Pylon
Trig point
Mast
Halkyn
Mountain
Windmill
Horse gin
Rhes-y-cae
Lime kilns
A55
Halkyn
Quarry
Fences
Masts
B5123
Wern-y-gaer
N
Moel y Gaer
Lime kiln
Rhosesmor
0
½ miles
0
500
1000 metres

agriculture and as an ingredient to make mortar. The lime used to be extracted from the rock using large kilns like the one you will see near the end of this walk.

2. Follow the path round to the head of the quarry; turn right by a slightly pointed stone fence pillar, along a path between gorse. After 40m, you reach rising ground to right and left – the ramparts of Moel y Gaer, an Iron Age hillfort.

The ramparts comprise a circular bank and an outer ditch, some 180m in diameter. With commanding views in every direction (it is worth walking a full circuit of the perimeter), this amazing feat of construction would have provided an excellent defence for its inhabitants some 2000-2500 years ago. A defendable site was needed because of increased competition for land. Archaeological excavation has shown that the hilltop was in use even earlier – in Neolithic time about 5500 years ago.

This is the highest point along these hills, some 303 metres/950 feet above sea level. The Clwydian Hills stretch off to your south-west, including Moel Famau with a 'blip' on top (actually the Jubilee Tower); and you can see the Pennines in the far distance to the east. (The raised, square area in the centre of the hillfort is a covered reservoir).

At Burton Point on Wirral there is also a defensive enclosure, thought to be Iron Age like Moel y Gaer's. However, it is only small, and its history is far less well understood than that of Moel y Gaer.

3. On the north-west side of the hillfort, find a path that runs downhill past an electricity pole about 30 metres from the ramparts. Descend and cross to a light-coloured track.

As you descend you notice the extraordinary pockmarked landscape. This is mining country and, since Roman times (maybe earlier), people have worked to extract lead and zinc that had formed in the fissures of the rock. Throughout this walk, you will pass hollows and mounds, the latter formed as people dumped spoil from their mining activity. The houses in the area are typically scattered, established by miners working on their chosen plots. The last mine closed in 1986.

The view from Moel y Gaer

4. Follow the track and it soon doubles back on itself to meet a road. Turn left along the road and continue to some terraced houses at the end. At the apex of the corner, continue ahead along a broad green path.
5. At the B5123, go left a few metres, then up the track to the right of the black and white chevron sign.
6. Walk between the two masts and the houses and continue, sometimes on a path, sometimes a track – your general direction is towards a single mast to the north-north-west.
7. At a road, take the signed route to 'Windmill'. Just before you reach the bungalow on the left, fork left off the road and walk alongside the bungalow's fence, still in the general direction of the mast. When you reach a track go left and follow it past the mast. Continue to the end and, 10m after the gate of Roseberry Villa, turn left to find a narrow path. It soon widens and passes between gorse, running just to the left of the highest pylon you can see in the distance. Continue in the general direction of the pylon.

8. 75m before the pylon, and just before a trig. point (the pyramidal concrete pillar) on a mound, you will shortly want to turn left down a clear path. First, however, take a walk up to the trig. point, to take in the excellent views.

You can pick out details of the Wirral, with the shining white houses of Parkgate particularly standing out. The less easily eroded limestone means that on this ridge you are always some 500' (160m) higher than any part of sandstone Wirral. Further away, Liverpool's cathedrals are clearly visible. Up the coast, you can make out Formby Point, and then Blackpool Tower. On a clear day, you can even make out the mountains of the Lake District some 75 miles away.

Trig. points were made as part of a process started in the 1930s to map the whole of the UK accurately. 6,173 were built and the job was not finished until 1962. My guess is that the most visited trig. point on the Wirral is on Thurstaston Hill.

With your back to the Wirral, look half right, down the hill, about 75 metres away. There are several excellent examples of 'bell-pits' – circular mounds made from the spoil being thrown out from a central mine shaft.

9. Take the path mentioned previously and go downhill. Ignore crossing paths (unless you want to visit the bell-pits) but fork left where the path splits just after a large horizontal slab of limestone to your right. The slabs are caps to old mine shafts; you can also find many beehive shaped stone cairns which cap the mines. You are aiming for the houses just visible to your half-left. Go straight over at cross-paths near bracken, eventually meeting the road opposite a playground at Rhes-y-cae. Walk along the right side of the playground.

Just overlapping the far right corner of the schoolyard you will find a 12m diameter grassy circular ditch. This was once a horse gin – a winding mechanism for the mines, powered by a horse walking round in circles, turning a large central pole with a rope wrapped around it.

10. Go left along the track and cross to a road, heading slightly uphill.

A miner's bell pit on the Common

150 metres after the junction turn right down a track between cottages (the left-hand one is called Fron Oleu). After the house on the left, as the track bends right, go ahead down a grassy path.

11. At the bottom of the hill, before the road, go left up a track. After about 250 metres, near a field corner to your right, turn right and follow the wire fence to find a stile hidden in the undergrowth. Cross it, and keep in the same direction to another stile. Continue in the same direction up a long grassy field, soon running parallel to another fence to reach a third stile at the top. Cross it and go straight ahead, then across a track, to join the road. Stay on this for 750m/½ mile, into Wern-y-gaer.

12. At a bend, by the black and white chevron sign, go straight ahead, along a narrow grassy path, parallel to a single line of cable. You reach a track to the left of a cream bungalow; go along this to meet a road. Turn left back to the start.

On your left is a limekiln. Rock was loaded through the hole on top

Lime kiln by Moel y Gaer

of the kiln and burnt at high temperatures. Lime was extracted which was then used in building and agriculture. Lime is an agricultural fertiliser and the kilns were a big factor in helping feed a rapidly growing population in the early 1800s.

Limekilns were also built on the Wirral – I know of ones at Little Neston and Thurstaston, though they were probably smaller than this one. Limestone would have been transported across the Dee from Wales by barge.

Walk 25. A Wirral Shore-to-Shore Trail: Parkgate to Eastham

– A fine route, right across the Wirral –

Start: The 'Donkey Stand' on The Parade at Parkgate (about 25 metres north of the Post Office).

Finish: Eastham Country Park Visitor Centre.

Transport: If possible, leave a car at the end or arrange to be met. Alternatively, plan around public transport routes that cross the trail – buses visit both ends. N.B. much of the route is suitable for cycles – use local maps to join the road and track sections together.

Distance: 10½ miles for the full walk. Otherwise, split the route into two or three sections for a series of outings.

Refreshments: Pubs and cafés at the start and finish, and at Willaston.

Walking Conditions: Generally very good paths and firm tracks. The short track at point 5 and the field at 7 can be muddy after rain. There is a short section of tunnel at point 12: you may like a torch but it is not essential.

Here's a fine challenge, to walk (or cycle) Wirral from shore to shore – from the Dee at Parkgate to the Mersey at Eastham. Along the way, we take in some of Wirral's finest countryside and beauty spots, including three Country Parks. With good paths and few hills, the walk is within most people's capabilities and would make a fine outing for country-lovers, families wanting a challenge or sponsored walkers seeking a novel route.

A tradition amongst coast-to-coast walkers is to touch the sea at either end of the walk. At Parkgate, with its rare high tides, the drainage gullies near the sea wall are your best option. At Eastham, Job's Ferry at high tide is best – but don't risk venturing onto the mud flats.

This route uses many of the paths discussed elsewhere in this book so, instead of duplicating information, I've cross-referenced to the relevant page(s). However, I have included information where the route covers new ground.

1. Walk south from the Donkey Stand and turn left up Station Road for 250 metres. Turn right at the 'Wirral Country Park' sign, going straight ahead at the top of the slope to join the Wirral Way (see pages 68 and 69) for 1.25km/¾ mile.

2. Shortly after the red metal Millennium Bridge, go straight ahead under the rail bridge and up a residential road. At the T-junction continue straight ahead, along the path (see page 124) for another 2.6km/1.6 miles. (Make sure you take the gate to the left immediately after going through the tunnel under the A540).

3. 200m after the pylon to the left, and shortly before a wooden gate, turn left, alongside a wire fence. *To visit Willaston's quaint Hadlow Road Station (see page122) restored to its 1950s look, stay on the Wirral Way for another 400 metres.*

   Join a gravel track, leading to the Pollard Inn car park. Walk down the drive to the right of the pub to emerge onto Willaston Green. *Pages 79 to 83 also cover this part of the shore-to-shore walk to just before point 6, with information and a short detour.*

4. Cross the main road, turn left for a few metres and turn right along the path just before the churchyard. When you reach a residential road, go half-left looking for a gap in the wall by the footpath sign. Take the path and, emerging at playing fields, keep to the right-hand boundary. Keep straight ahead for about 450 metres going through a gate and crossing stiles. Reach a road, and turn right.

5. After 150 metres turn left along a track, signposted to Raby. After another 150 metres turn right across stone steps and a stile. Walk gently downhill, with the field boundary to your left. Keep straight ahead for about 1km (0.6 miles), crossing stiles and footbridges.

6. Emerge at Benty Heath Lane. Turn left and walk for 350 metres. As the road bends left turn right, along a lane with a footpath sign, past brick cottages.

The Wirral Way (Photograph: Cheshire County Council)

7. Immediately after crossing the motorway turn left and walk along the field edge. At a stile cross and turn right to reach a golf course. Cross the fairway and stay on this heading following white marker posts.

8. Reaching a stile at Raby Hall Road turn right for 75m, then go left along Blakeley Road, and walk to Raby Mere (page 37).

9. Descend Poulton Hall Road, and continue, to climb out of the valley (caution – the road is narrow here). At the T-junction look for a 'Public Footpath' sign across fields, and pass a telegraph pole.

10. At the field corner, follow the main path. After a few metres, as the view opens up across the valley of Dibbensdale and 10 metres before a bench, fork left down a faint path. 75 metres later go hard right, almost doubling back, and descend the hill. Towards the foot of the hill, at the main path, turn left.

Dibbinsdale Local Nature Reserve has much natural interest, containing woodland, meadows, reed swamps, parkland and grassland. Dibbinsdale Wood is especially important as it is believed to be the largest area of 'ancient woodland' on Merseyside i.e. land that's been continually wooded since trees started growing after the last ice age. Trees here today include ash and wych elm, which once dominated the woodland. There are also oak, sycamore, beech, and hornbeam. Dibbinsdale has been designated a Site of Special Scientific Interest.

11. Cross two bridges over the stream. 20 metres after the second, bend left along the main path.

On the right, just before a bench at a point marked '7' are two hornbeams, an uncommon tree this far north, with grey-green rippled bark.

12. At a railway, ignore the steps; go through a tunnel, named 'Otter Bridge'.

The bridge was named by workmen building the railway embankment in the late 1830s who saw many otters playing here. Sadly, none have been seen since the 1863. Keep an eye open for kingfishers along the stream though.

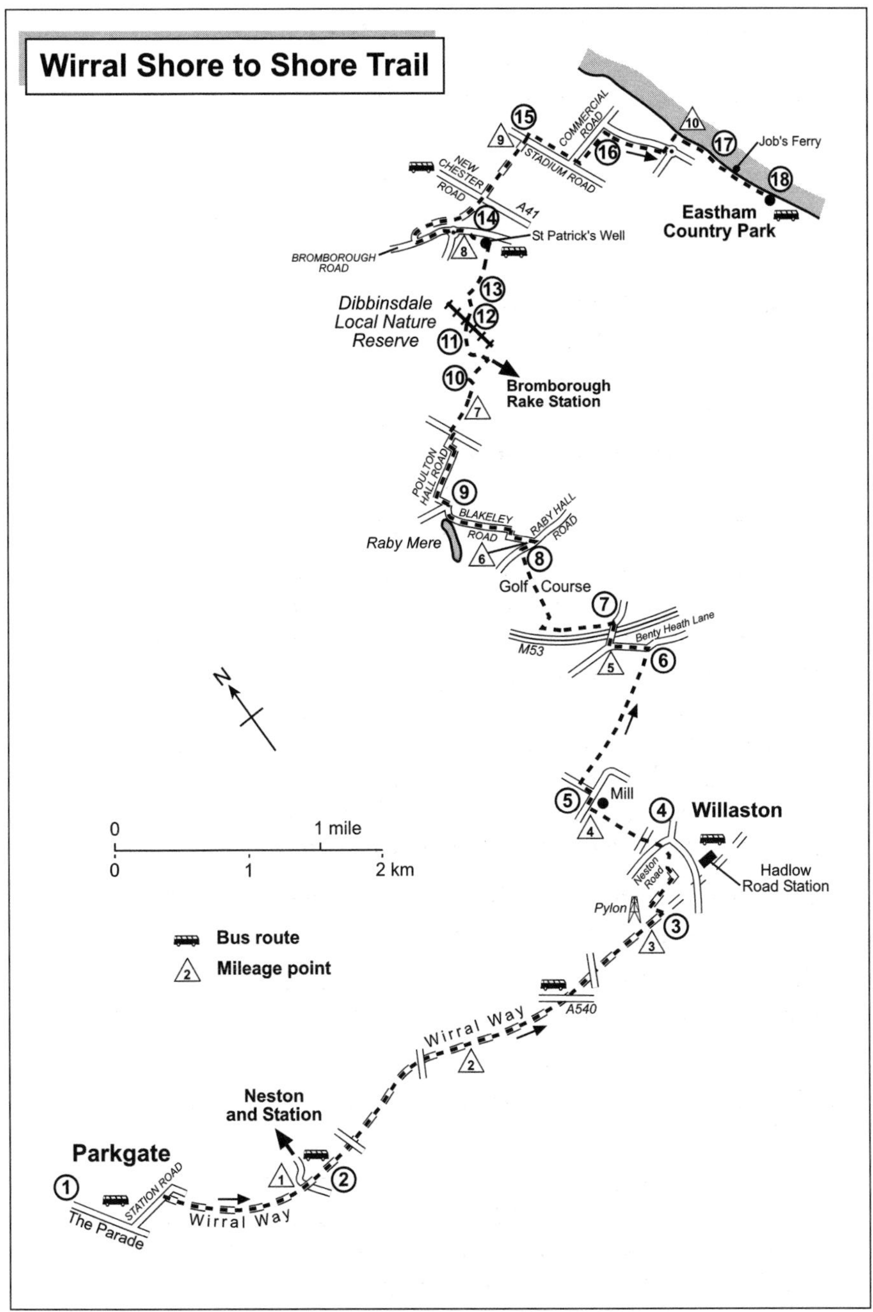
Wirral Shore to Shore Trail
Job's Ferry
Eastham Country Park
COMMERCIAL ROAD
STADIUM ROAD
NEW CHESTER ROAD
A41
St Patrick's Well
BROMBOROUGH ROAD
Dibbinsdale Local Nature Reserve
Bromborough Rake Station
POULTON HALL ROAD
BLAKELEY ROAD
RABY HALL ROAD
Raby Mere
Golf Course
Benty Heath Lane
M53
Mill
Willaston
Neston Road
Hadlow Road Station
Pylon
A540
Wirral Way
Neston and Station
Parkgate
STATION ROAD
The Parade
Wirral Way
0
1 mile
0
1
2 km
Bus route
Mileage point

13. Stick to the main path, passing stands of common reed (traditionally grown in eastern England for thatching roofs) to reach another bridge. A few metres later, take the right-hand path uphill; 100 metres later, at a junction, go straight ahead, initially downhill.

Soon you reach a good viewpoint over the river and beyond. The 'carr woodland' around the valley bottom, which is regularly flooded, includes willow, alder and dogwood.

Continue; 75 metres later, take the left-hand, lesser, path along the top of the bank. At the bottom of the hill, when you meet other main paths, look out for St Patrick's Well to your right.

The well is said to have been blessed by Saint Patrick in the fifth century AD and the waters are supposed to have healing powers for the eyes.

14. At the road turn left, and go straight ahead at the mini-roundabout, passing a World War II pillbox. Notice the 13 metre high embankment to your right, over the River Dibbin at Spital Dam (Incidentally the name 'Spital' comes from a nearby lepers' 'ho-*spital*' in the Middle Ages). Walk uphill for 300m. At railings turn right through a gap in the wall and join the Cycleway/Footpath for 1km (0.6 miles).

The rest of the route, until you reach the boundary of Eastham Country Park, has, perhaps, a surprising significance. It follows almost precisely the line of railways constructed by Lever Brothers from 1910 to link their factories at Port Sunlight and Bromborough Port, and to give access to docks on the Mersey and to the main Birkenhead – Chester railway line. Numerous branch lines came off the route and even the right-hand turns that our walking route makes mirror the many turns made by the railways.

The route soon goes over the embankment you saw earlier. Soon you enter a cutting that is 9 metres deep, passing under the New Chester Road.